Gift from Richard
December 1972

THE NEW WORLD OF NEEDLEPOINT

Random House, New York

THE NEW WORLD OF NEEDLEPOINT

101 Exciting Designs in Bargello, Quickpoint, Grospoint, and Other Repeat Patterns

LISBETH PERRONE

Library of Congress Cataloging in Publication Data
Perrone, Lisbeth.   The new world of needlepoint.
1. Canvas embroidery. I. Title.
TT778.C3P47   746.4′4   72-3086   ISBN 0-394-47265-9

Manufactured in the United States of America

Design by Kenneth Miyamoto
Photographs by Steve Wasserman
Type set by The Poole Clarinda Company
Printed and bound by Kingsport Press, Kingsport, Tenn.

98765432

FIRST EDITION

ACKNOWLEDGMENTS

I WOULD LIKE to extend my thanks and deep appreciation to Louise
Miller and Joan von Albrecht, who have been of invaluable help in
executing the patterns in this book; to all my students, past and
present; to those who gave me permission to publish photographs of
their work, particularly Joan von Albrecht for the use of her sampler
on page 8 and *Redbook* Magazine for the use on the same page of the
photograph of the footstool I designed for them; to Mrs. Daryl
Parshall of Millbrook, N.Y., who let me adapt some patterns from an
old sampler which is in her possession; and to the Embroiderers'
Guild of America, Inc., in whose library I spent many lovely hours.

To Philip, and our son, Abbott

A very quaint writer once said: "No female character can be quite perfect without a knowledge of all sorts of needlework, and a downright hearty lot of it too, and many a heartache has been buried in the growing petals of a silken rose, and the sharp edge of sorrow been dulled by the sweet, calm monotony of a shining bit of steel."

CONTENTS

INTRODUCTION

ANYONE WHO has ever done needlepoint knows how easy it is. This book is a handbook of 101 of my own favorite canvas embroidery designs, including Bargello, quickpoint, grospoint and many other repeat patterns. To do any one of them, you need to know only the five simple stitches explained at the beginning of the book. In fact, many of you probably know these stitches already.

As you will see, you can use the patterns separately or combined to make all sorts of things: cushions, chair seats, headbands, belts, wallets, pincushions, wall hangings. Most of the designs are original; they are as unusual and as beautiful as I have been able to make them.

To do these patterns you don't have to buy expensive painted canvases and you are not restricted to what is supplied to you in a commercial kit. Naturally, you will save money when you use this method, but just as important, you will have the chance to do something that is especially yours. I think you will find that canvas embroidery will become a pleasant and inexpensive part of your life once you begin to work with this book. (In fact, the only complaint I've had about the designs is that you have to be careful that working them doesn't become an overwhelming passion.)

The book is not an encyclopedia of canvas embroidery, a dictionary of stitches, or a manual for finishing your work at home. Rather, it is arranged to show you colored photographs of all the patterns as I have worked them. Then, each design appears on a separate page in a detailed photograph, together with an easy-to-follow work chart. At the top of each page I have noted whether the design is easy, intermediate, or advanced. Of course, try the easy ones first if you are a beginner, but you will find that you will advance very quickly to become a skilled embroiderer. And that is a very lovely thing to be.

Canvas embroidery is done all over the world and it has a very long history. Until almost into the twentieth century, much of a woman's earliest education was needlework. It was considered more important to be an accomplished needlewoman than to read or write. Today both men and women embroider for pleasure and as a recreation, but in the past women embroidered out of necessity, to make many functional furnishings and coverings for their homes.

Each era and each country has added something new to the craft, until today, with the rich variety of yarns and colors available, it is possible to create a multitude of exciting contemporary and traditional designs and patterns. You will find that canvas embroidery is fun, easy, soothing—and beautifully creative.

WHAT IS CANVAS EMBROIDERY?

Canvas embroidery, or needlepoint, includes all kinds of embroidery done on a single- or double-mesh canvas—Bargello, or Florentine, embroidery, quickpoint, grospoint, petitpoint and other repeat patterns.

1. **Bargello.** Bargello is also known as Florentine, flame or Hungarian embroidery. It is usually done in a straight vertical stitch, covering more than one canvas thread at a time. The stitch is worked across the canvas. By varying the number of threads covered, curves and peaks can be formed ingeniously. The count has to be very accurate in Bargello embroidery, but that is nothing to worry about, because once a single horizontal line has been established, the other rows fall easily into place. Though the stitch is usually worked over more than one canvas thread, the size of the stitch frequently remains constant throughout the pattern.

2. **Petitpoint.** Petitpoint, a time-consuming and exacting technique, is done primarily in the continental or basket-weave stitch on canvas with more than 20 canvas threads to the inch. None of the patterns in this book have been worked in petitpoint, but any of the grospoint patterns are suitable for petitpoint work. Just use a finer canvas and a finer yarn.

3. **Grospoint.** Grospoint is usually done in the continental or basket-weave stitch, but a coarser canvas is used—less than 20 canvas threads to the inch. Whether we call this type of work petitpoint or grospoint is just a matter of size of the mesh of the canvas.

4. **Quickpoint.** Quickpoint has become very popular within the last few years for very good reasons: it is quick to work up, easy to count and is an excellent way to begin to learn the various stitches and patterns. Quickpoint is done on a very coarse canvas, varying in size from 3 threads to 7 threads to the inch. There is no special quickpoint stitch; what identifies it is the coarse canvas and heavy yarn that are used. It can be a Bargello pattern, a basket-weave or a continental stitch. In this book, all quickpoint patterns were done with Paternayan rug wool or DMC quickpoint yarn.

It is sometimes difficult to find the right weight quickpoint yarn (rug wool), though many stores will order it for you. If you are having trouble, buy a very good quality heavy pure-wool knitting yarn. However, before you buy this wool in large quantity, experiment with it on your quickpoint canvas. The canvas thread may show a bit, but bear in mind that because you are using so fluffy a yarn, it will flatten down, especially after you've blocked it. Even so, in very bold, straight-stitched patterns, it is a good idea to paint your canvas before you begin your work (see page 12).

5. **Repeat patterns.** All patterns in this book are technically repeat patterns. Each pattern has a motif or structure which can be repeated on the canvas. The number of repeats in your finished work depends on the size of your project. Thus, though the patterns are shown in this book in small sample squares, you can, of course, use them to make any shape or size you like.

WHAT TOOLS AND MATERIALS ARE NEEDED?

1. A **basket** or some other storage unit in which to keep your materials is a great help. You will find that if all your needlework equipment is not kept in one place, one thing or another will always be missing.

2. **Needles** used for canvas embroidery are strong and have a blunt end. The eye of the needle should be large enough so that the yarn pulls through with ease, without fraying. A simple rule to remember is to pick a needle whose eye is a bit wider than the yarn is thick. Needles are identified by numbers, and those most commonly used for the Persian or tapestry yarn available are #18, #19 and #20. However, for quickpoint, which is done with a heavier yarn, use a blunt-ended darning needle. Never embroider with a bent or rusty needle. You will end up with frayed yarn or an uneven piece of work.

3. Keep two sets of **scissors** in your embroidery basket: a heavy pair for cutting canvas or skeins of yarn and a small pointed pair for cutting yarn or—if worse comes to worst—for ripping a mistake. (A really valuable tool is the kind of "**ripper**" that is available in notions stores or places that sell sewing machines.)

4. A **thimble** is a very personal thing. Some people cannot do without it, and some cannot do with it. I don't believe that one way is superior to the other. However, if you do like to work with a thimble, it should be deep and fairly rounded.

5. The **yarns** I used throughout this book are Paternayan 3-ply Persian-type yarn, DMC 4-ply tapestry yarn and quickpoint yarn (rug wool). The 3-ply loosely twisted Persian-type yarn has the advantage that you can easily add or subtract a strand or two and mix shades in this fashion. One strand only is usually used for petitpoint. Even a thin strand of silver or gold mixed in with your yarn will highlight the embroidery in a very dramatic way. The two types, Persian and tapestry, can be used interchangeably or together on the

same canvas. As a matter of fact, if you do not overdo it, mixing textures of yarn will give you a more interesting finished piece.

Quickpoint yarn is available in several weights, and in mixtures of wool and man-made fibers. Whenever possible, try to buy the fluffiest pure-wool rug yarn available. The Paternayan rug wool and the DMC quickpoint yarn work very well.

If possible, avoid knitting yarn, since it has a tendency to stretch. However, as we have seen, it is sometimes difficult to get a good fluffy quickpoint yarn, in which case, the only solution is a knitting yarn.

The canvas should be completely covered, and for this reason, it is important that there be a good relationship between the canvas and the yarn used. If the yarn is too thick, it will pull the canvas out of shape, and if the yarn is too thin, the canvas will show through. One stitch or pattern will use more yarn than another. A vertical or horizontal stitch usually requires more and thicker yarn than a slanted stitch. It is therefore advisable to start a new pattern with a sampler, so that you can see what size canvas and what kind and quantity of yarn it takes for a given size stitch or pattern.

Next, go to your yarn shop with the pattern, the specifications of yarn, canvas size and the number of colors described in the book. The clerk will usually be able to tell you how many ounces of yarn to use. Otherwise, you can very roughly and generously figure 6 ounces for a 10-inch by 10-inch project. It is better to buy a little more yarn than is called for, since most stores will allow you to return the unused portion. That way, you won't have to worry about matching dye lots if you run out.

6. **Canvas** can be obtained in linen or cotton. If you can get it, I recommend linen because it is more durable. White canvas is easiest to find, but canvas sometimes is available in ecru. If you are working with long, straight stitches, it is better to work on an ecru canvas where there is less chance of the canvas thread showing through. Sometimes when you are working a pattern with straight stitches, the white canvas will show through even if you have selected the right weight wool. If you notice this on your sampler, coat your canvas with an acrylic or oil-base paint in a color that more or less matches your yarns.

Canvas comes in widths from 18 to 54 inches, and is usually purchased by the yard. It is available in coarseness graded from #3 to #28. The lower the number, the coarser the canvas. The coarseness is measured by how many woven threads there are to the inch. For example, #12 canvas has 12 threads to the inch. The kind of canvas you choose will depend upon what kind of yarn and which pattern or stitch you select. For every pattern in the book, I have indicated the number of the canvas and the type of yarn to be used.

Note that I have used #5 canvas for all quickpoint patterns. Your local supplier may call this rug canvas or quickpoint canvas and he may carry only a somewhat coarser or finer mesh. Just test your yarn in relation to the available canvas.

Canvas is available in double or single mesh. The double-mesh canvas (sometimes referred to as Penelope) is a bit more restricting than the single mesh because you can't work all patterns on it. Also, many embroiderers find the double mesh confusing and a strain to the eye. However, since the quickpoint canvases are hard to find in single mesh, we have worked all of these on double-mesh canvas.

Do not buy—or even accept free—any canvas that has knots or uneven threads in it. It is of inferior quality, will be hard to work and will give poor results.

7. The edges of the canvas should be bound with **masking tape**. The tape will keep your canvas from raveling. When you block or clean the finished piece, tacks can be placed on the taped edge rather than on the canvas or the embroidered part. More important, if the edges are not taped, the yarn will constantly catch the rough edges and will fray or break.

8. A good trick to keep your yarn in order is to buy an **embroidery hoop** in wood or metal. Then, if the yarn does not come in a pull skein, braid the loose bundle around the hoop in an old-fashioned braid, with the ends hanging free. (See photograph, page 19.) This allows you to pull one strand of wool at a time. The braid will remain intact and keep the yarn in order.

9. Don't buy a **frame** unless the project is very large. Canvas embroidery is almost always worked in the hand and is therefore very convenient for the embroiderer to pick up, store and carry around. However, if you have a tendency to pull your stitches too tightly, a frame may help you work more evenly.

10. A **notebook** is imperative. You will find it so useful that you will wonder how you ever did without it. Ideas come and go and — at least for me — if they are not recorded, they are lost forever. In your notebook, you can record hints and suggestions from other embroiderers, sources of supply and, most important, the size canvas, the kind of yarn and the amount used for a given stitch or pattern.

11. You will find a **permanent-ink felt pen** useful for marking the center of your design and indicating the outlines of your project. There are many of these pens on the market, but some are of inferior quality and the ink may run when the piece is blocked. A felt-tip illustrator's pen will not run, and that is the kind I use in my own work.

THE STITCHES

The Continental Stitch. The continental is a slanted stitch that is always worked from the right side of the canvas to the left. *All the stitches go in the same direction* (see diagram, far right). When one row is completed, turn the canvas around and come back, working from right to left again. I do not recommend this stitch to cover large areas, since it is likely to pull the canvas out of shape.

There will be times when you will find it necessary to work the continental in a vertical line. In this case, do not work from right to left, but from top to bottom (see diagram, near right).

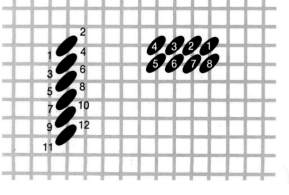

The Basket-Weave or **Diagonal Stitch.** Basket-weave is a very sturdy stitch that usually does not pull the canvas and is appropriate for large background areas. Though the instructions sound complicated, basket-weave is really worth learning. However, bear in mind that the basket-weave stitch can be used with *or* instead of the continental stitch, since they look exactly the same on the front of the canvas. Don't get discouraged if you can't grasp this stitch at first. Come back to it when you have the time to experiment.

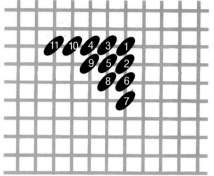

This stitch is *not* worked horizontally. It is always worked in diagonal rows, with all the stitches in the same direction. Study the diagram carefully and you will see that the stitches on each row cover *every other* diagonal crossing of the canvas. Then the returning diagonal row fills in the alternate canvas crossings. (See numbers on diagram.)

To begin this work, first establish two ordinary continental stitches (1 and 2 on the diagram) one right beneath the other. Now work 3 and 4. You have now established a corner. Next, work 5 and 6 to establish the regular diagonal line of the basket-weave stitch.

Move from row to row in this manner, adding or subtracting a stitch at the end of the line if you need to change the size of the work. Always work the stitch diagonally back and forth, back and forth, without turning the canvas. Thus, when you take a new thread, start at exactly the place you left off.

The Cross-Stitch. Most of the cross-stitches in this book are worked over one or two canvas threads. If the pattern calls for a number of cross-stitches, make sure the top stitches of all the crosses go in the same direction (see diagram at right).

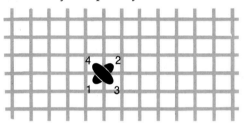

The French Knot. French knots have to be firm and neat so that they will not move out of place. Carry the needle up from the back of the canvas. Hold the needle in your right hand. Wind the yarn around the needle with your left hand, as close to the canvas as possible. Keep the yarn taut and lower the needle through the adjacent hole. (Never wind the yarn more than twice around the needle. If you want a heavier knot, use a double strand of yarn.) Please note that in the work charts most French knots are shown in the canvas squares where they finally fall rather than in the holes through which the needle goes (see diagram at left).

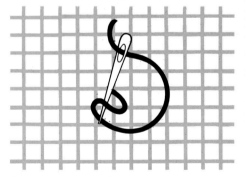

The Florentine Stitch (Bargello, Hungarian, or **Flame Stitch).** Work in straight vertical lines in the sequence (1, 2, 3, etc.) noted on the diagram. Don't take shortcuts with the yarn from one place on the canvas to another. The more

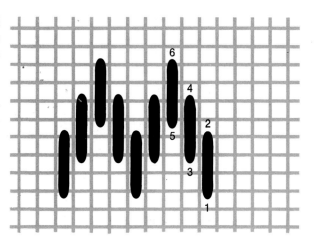

yarn on the back of this kind of work, the stronger the finished piece will be. The Florentine stitch usually covers the same number of canvas threads throughout a pattern to form diamonds, curves and peaks. Work horizontally back and forth across the canvas unless otherwise indicated. Note that adjoining rows of this stitch *always* share the same holes in the canvas.

HOW TO SELECT A DESIGN

The first question to ask yourself in selecting a design is: what kind of finished piece do I want to come out with? It could be anything from a headband to a large wall hanging, but if you have not done much embroidery before, choose a project that is modest in size. When you are a beginner, it is more rewarding to make a few small pieces than one large one that takes a long time to finish. Everybody needs all the encouragement he or she can get when starting a new venture, and what is more encouraging than the satisfaction of having a few beautiful finished pieces? Pincushions, for example, make wonderful gifts, and—they're tiny.

For small projects, pick a pattern that has a small repeat. For larger work, you can use either a bold design or a fine one. For a finished piece that will get a lot of wear, pick a pattern with small stitches rather than one which has long stitches, covering many canvas threads.

Look through the full-color photographs until you find a pattern you like. A few elaborately colored patterns appear on the same page as their instructions. Otherwise, look at the page number next to the pattern you're considering. Turn to that page. You will find it is completely devoted to that particular pattern, with a photograph of the design, a work chart and instructions. Each pattern is coded at the top of the page as to whether it is easy, intermediate or advanced. However, don't take these designations too seriously. If you have already done canvas embroidery, you will find most of the patterns easy.

Don't be afraid to change the colors that are shown here. If you see a design that you love that is worked in orange and green, and your living room is in pale pinks and blues, just change the colors. Use your notebook to keep a record of what you're doing, and you shouldn't have any difficulty at all.

For your first solo attempts at color mixing, monochromatic combinations are safest. That is, use several shades of one color—blue, for example—with perhaps black or gray or white as a highlight. Later on, when you get more confident, you can use any color combination that pleases your eye. Of course, you need to keep in mind where the finished piece is going to be placed. It should be part of its environment, neither too dominant nor too timid.

You should feel the same freedom about changing an element you don't like in a particular design. For example, if you find a pattern that strikes your fancy except for the French knots at the corners, substitute cross-stitches or some other device. Simply count carefully and keep track of what you've done in your notebook.

The other easy conversion you can make is in the scale of the pattern. If you like a pattern shown in grospoint, but you want a bolder look—*and* work that goes quickly—you can work most patterns on a #5 canvas with a quickpoint yarn. Also, remember that you can always substitute 3-ply Persian-type yarn for 4-ply tapestry yarn, and vice versa.

HOW TO READ A CHART

Now that you have selected a design, you will be living on the page devoted to it. First, consider whether it is **easy, intermediate** or **advanced**, and then look at the type **canvas** and **yarn** which are to be used and how many **colors** you will need. Any special problems of the design or possible uses for this particular pattern will be explained in the instructions.

The **photograph** is to help you visualize the pattern as you are working it. When it is necessary, the photograph will indicate the **detail** that the chart represents.

The grid of each work **chart** represents your canvas, and the lines or symbols drawn on the grid represent individual stitches. Most charts show one full motif, which is to be repeated as often as you need in order to complete the canvas you are working. Some motifs take up so much room that the chart can show only half the pattern. In these cases, the instructions will indicate that to continue the pattern, you work in a mirror image.

There are two types of charts:

1. The charts for patterns executed in the continental or basket-weave stitch are done with symbols. Each symbol represents one stitch worked in a particular color. A change of symbol indicates *only* a change in color. Next to each of these charts is a color key showing which color each symbol represents. For example: ▲ = blue, ╱ = yellow.

2. The charts for other designs are drawn with horizontal, vertical or slanted lines in different tones of blue and black.* (In some cases, full-color charts are

---

*In a few instances an advanced pattern may combine straight stitches and continental or basket-weave stitches. In these cases, the background is not shown on the chart. It is always done in the basket-weave or continental stitch.

shown.) Don't be confused about this. The tones of the lines in the charts do not represent the *actual* colors, but are used to make it easy for you to see how many colors there are and when to start a new color. Where we have used, for example, 4 tones, the design then calls for 4 different colors; 3 tones indicate 3 colors, 8 tones indicate 8 colors, etc. You can easily refer back to the color photograph of the pattern if you need to, or you can use the black-and-white photograph above the chart to follow the color changes.

When you are working with a pattern that has more than three or four colors, you may find it helpful to use your notebook to keep track. However, once the pattern line is established, you should have no trouble.

Each line on the grid represents the actual size of your stitch. That is, a stitch going over 3 lines of the grid means the yarn must go over 3 threads of your canvas. When counting the size of the stitch, *never* count the holes on the grid or canvas. Always count the lines or threads. This is true for all canvas patterns.

Note that all patterns show 2 stitches coming out of the same hole or square of the grid. Follow this exactly, or you will come out with an empty space on your canvas. French knots are shown on the charts in the squares between the canvas thread. However, this only indicates the place the knots should fall. Of course, the needle goes down again in an adjacent square. (See instruction for French knots on page 14.)

In looking at a new chart, don't try to figure out the whole pattern at once simply by observation. Instead, get your needle and yarn out and, step by step, work the pattern up in a sampler, counting with the chart. Counting threads and following a chart may sound difficult to the beginner, but you will find that the pattern is established very quickly in almost every design, and then it really follows itself. The chart becomes only a reference, like a map you turn to from time to time on an automobile trip when you change directions.

HOW TO WORK A PROJECT

You are now ready to cut your canvas. Lay it out on a flat, clean surface. Don't worry about what direction to turn it. On the type of canvas used in this book, monocanvas, there is no top or bottom, no right or wrong side.

Remember to cut the canvas at least 2 inches extra on all sides to allow for blocking and mounting. In other words, if you are making a pillow 12 inches by 12 inches, cut the canvas 16 inches by 16 inches. If you are making an eyeglass case, a belt or a clutch bag, make a paper pattern in the shape you want, lay it on the canvas and, again, allow 2 extra inches all around when you cut the canvas. Then indicate the actual size of your project on the cut canvas.

Next, put masking tape around the edges of the canvas and, with your permanent pen, mark the center of the canvas as well as the outline, or all the corners, of what is going to be the actual size of the finished piece.

To find the center, first lightly fold the canvas in half horizontally, then in half vertically. Where the two folds intersect, place a straight pin. You now have the center of the canvas.

Remember to start the center of the pattern in the center of the canvas so that the repeats will be evenly distributed on the finished piece. When there are diagonal designs, the instructions will remind you to work on the diagonal. Otherwise, work in horizontal or vertical lines out from the center.

Now go back and look at the pattern you have selected and see how many colors are going to be used. Allow each color yarn its own needle. It is easier to work with a few needles than to have to rethread one needle every time you change colors.

Never knot your yarn. When you are just beginning your work, leave a strand of about 2 inches hanging loose in the back. Then, after you have completed a portion of work, you can weave the dangling thread into the stitches on the back of the canvas.

Fasten the beginning and the end of the yarn by weaving it in and out of the stitches already on

the back. It is very important to fasten the yarn securely in canvas embroidery, since you are working with an open mesh material and the yarn can pull out easily.

You can carry one color yarn from one place to another in the pattern across the back of the canvas, provided the distance is not more than 1 inch. If the yarn has to stretch longer than that, fasten it and start again in the new place on the pattern. Don't take shortcuts with your yarn to get from place to place on the back of the canvas. The more yarn you use to cover the back, the sturdier your piece. Don't pull the yarn too taut.

Never work with a piece of yarn longer than 18 inches. Work with an even tension. Don't pull the yarn too tight or let it go too slack. Sometimes a strand of yarn will be twisted and your work will look uneven. If that happens, hold your canvas up in the air and let the threaded needle hang straight down in a vertical line. It will unwind itself the way a telephone cord does.

In every pattern, you will see that more than one strand of wool will meet in each hole. Make sure the yarn is taut enough so that it doesn't interfere with the previous stitch. When you're working with more than one needle, bring the needles not in use up to the top of the embroidery so they don't get entangled in your work.

Follow the chart and the photograph carefully until you are feeling very familiar with the pattern. Watch especially closely when you are making squared-off corners and when you are working a finely detailed pattern in the continental stitch. However, despite these precautions, bear in mind that once you establish one motif of the pattern, the rest will fall into place.

Don't rush your work. Canvas embroidery is not a job for which you are getting paid piecework, but is a pleasant way to occupy yourself. If you let it become a chore and rush through the designs, you won't get the fun out of it that you should and you will make mistakes. Finally, take good care of your finished embroidery. If the piece is going to have functional use, it is advisable to Scotchgard it. Now and then, when it has become part of your life, brush the finished needlework gently with a soft brush.

HOW TO FINISH AN EMBROIDERED PIECE

As we have seen, all sorts of things can be made with canvas embroidery—pillows, pictures, footstools, chair seats, bell-pulls, bookends, wall hangings, mirror frames, picture frames, table tops, coasters, handbags, luggage racks, vests, belts, headbands, eyeglass cases, pincushions, bookmarks and all the other uses you are going to invent yourself.

In order to complete the piece, three basic steps are necessary: checking the work, blocking and mounting.

First **check** the work carefully. Hold it up to the light to make sure that the canvas is completely and evenly covered. Take a careful look at the design to catch any glaring errors you have made. (It's a good idea to save some yarn in each of the colors for repair purposes.)

Make sure all threads are securely fastened. Trim the back of your embroidery, clipping unnecessarily long threads (though not too close to the canvas).

Now it is time to block, if necessary. Many of the patterns shown in this book do not require blocking. Block only if the canvas is pulled out of shape—which will sometimes happen with the continental stitch or when all the stitches in a pattern go in one direction. Do not press your work, as this will flatten it.

To **block**, place the canvas, embroidery face-down, on a clean surface. With a wet sponge, go over the back lightly, until the piece is damp. Sponge only the part of the canvas which is embroidered. If the front of the embroidery is soiled, lightly sponge the embroidered surface. Never use harsh detergents or chemicals which might break the dye of the yarn.

While the piece is still damp, attach it to a flat board, a stretcher board or an old table. Have on hand rust-proof carpet tacks or push-pins. Tack the four corners of the embroidery first, pulling the canvas taut enough to create a bit of tension between the tacks. Then push four more tacks into the board, one in the center of each side. Continue this way until the edges are covered with tacks, about 1/4 inch apart. Allow the canvas to dry at least 24 hours.

When the piece is thoroughly dry, it is a good idea to spray on a coat of Scotchgard, following the directions on the spray can. This will help make it stain and soil-resistant.

You are now ready to **mount** your work. You can have a professional do this job for you, but it is sometimes a very expensive procedure. (My own local dry cleaner does an excellent job for a reasonable price, as does the upholsterer in my neighborhood.) These instructions are for a few simple objects you can make yourself. However, if you feel nervous about mounting your work, there are several very good books on the market devoted exclusively to finishing a piece of embroidery.

To **mount** your own work, buy a piece of fabric that goes well with the colors of your embroidery. Cut a paper pattern the same size as your canvas (2 inches larger than the embroidered portion). Pin the paper pattern to the cloth. Cut the cloth, then stitch it by hand to the reverse side, along the edge of the embroidery on your finished canvas. (Thus, the top of your embroidery faces the right side of the fabric.)

To make a **pillow** or a **pincushion**, stitch three sides of the fabric and the embroidery together, leaving one edge open so you can reverse and then close the piece. The last side of your pillow will have to be stitched by hand after the piece is finished and the stuffing is in place. Make sure that the inner pillow you use for your embroidery is stuffed with good quality material, such as down or dacron. It is a pity to spoil a piece you've worked long and hard on by finishing it with shoddy stuff.

To make a **belt**, an **eyeglass case**, a **bookmark** or a **headband**, follow the same procedure as for pillows and pincushions, omitting the stuffing, of course. Back the embroidery with a sturdy fabric in a good color. You can, if you like, also use a stiffener, such as buckram, between the embroidery and the backing. I don't usually bother with this step.

To make a **picture** of your embroidered piece, stretch and attach the finished canvas to an artist's board of heavy cardboard or to a very thin piece of plywood. To do this, cut the board to exactly the size of the embroidered portion of your work. Then wrap the unembroidered edges of the canvas around to the back side of the board. Fasten them down with a very heavy grade adhesive tape or with a fine quality transparent adhesive or glue. Then simply slide the covered board into one of the excellent assemble-yourself picture frames that are available in any art supply or department store.

Since canvas embroidery is a heavy, rather stiff medium, you obviously should use it only to make clothing with simple lines. Actually, I have only made vests out of this kind of work.

To make a **vest**, or any other straight piece of clothing, buy a commercial pattern in the dress pattern department of your local store. Before you begin your embroidery, lay the pattern on the canvas and cut the canvas as you would any fabric. However, leave 3 inches all around for blocking and fitting. Then work your embroidery, and assemble. It is important to line all clothing made from canvas embroidery.

If you want to make a **heavy-duty handbag**, go to a professional, who will give you the proper dimensions and then line and mount the piece for you. However, you can make a simple **envelope bag** by cutting a straight piece of canvas to the size you want. Line the finished work, fold it to form the body and flap of the purse and then stitch it into place.

Chair seats covered with canvas embroidery last forever. In this case, though it is fairly expensive, get your local upholsterer to mount the canvas for you. You will find that you have made an excellent lifetime investment.

THE DESIGNS

page 24

page 25

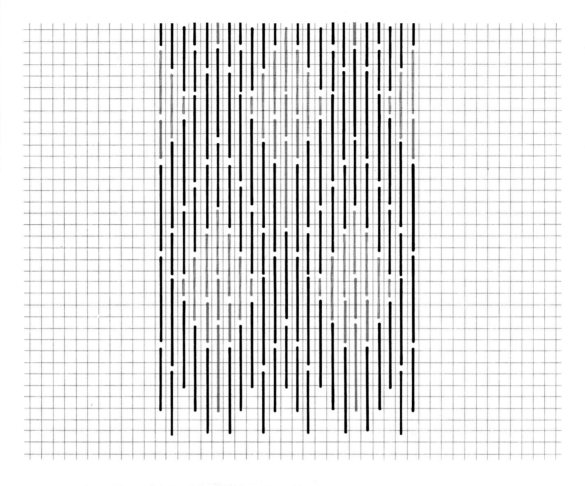

**#10 Canvas
3-ply Persian-type Yarn
4 Colors**

In these colors this is a
delicious-looking, crisp
design. First work the
"V-shapes" horizontally
across the canvas. Then
fill in the little trees
at the centers.

Color Illustration, page 23

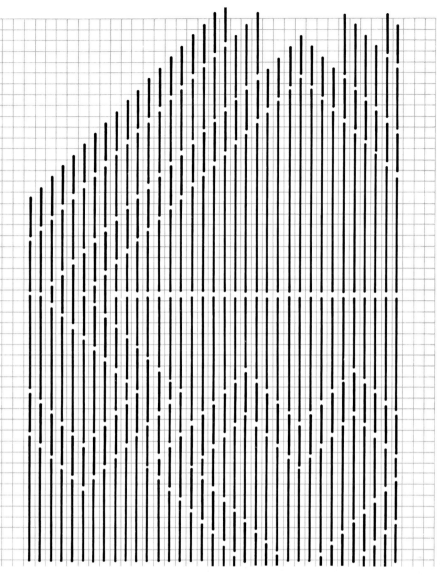

#12 Canvas
3-ply Persian-type Yarn
2 Colors

A very simple-looking, elegant design with very long stitches, not suitable for functional use. It would make a beautiful screen or large wall hanging. Note that the pattern reverses itself, and therefore requires very accurate counting. To move from the repeat shown here, work in a mirror image. A beginner should not attempt this one.

Color Illustration, page 23

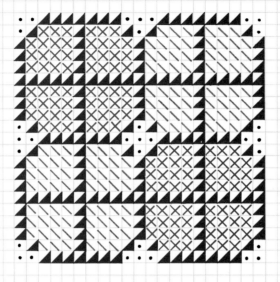

#5 Canvas
Quickpoint Yarn
4 Colors

Done in the continental
or basket-weave stitch,
this pattern has a stained-
glass effect. Work up the
frames first and then fill
in the little windows.

◤ = green
• = yellow
✕ = fuchsia
╲ = pink

#12 Canvas
3-ply Persian Yarn
5 Colors

This is my editor's favorite pattern. It would make a really beautiful chair or other large piece that would benefit from the display of four or more repeats. Start at the center, working the star in a straight stitch. Then work the pale-blue framework, also in a straight stitch. Now all you have to do is fill in the navy-blue and white background areas in the continental or basket-weave stitch. Note carefully that the diagram shows a little more than one-fourth the motif. To continue, work in a mirror image.

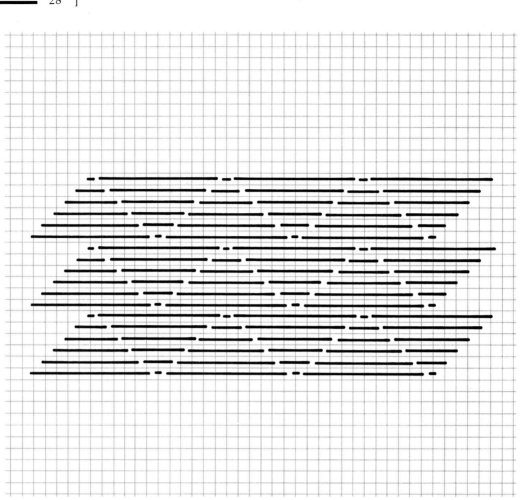

**#10 Canvas
3-ply Persian-type Yarn
2 Colors**

The base of each triangle
meets the peak of the
triangle above or below
it. In other words, reverse
the triangles, one row
turned up and one
turned down.

Color Illustration, page 30

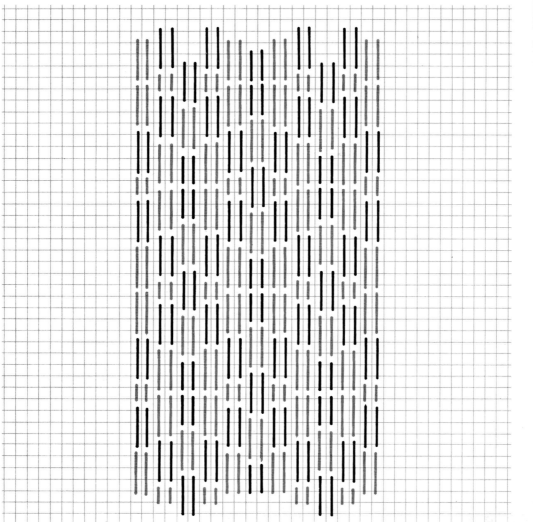

#10 Canvas
3-ply Persian-type Yarn
3 Colors

This is a diamond-shaped Bargello pattern. First establish the diagonal outlines for the diamonds, then fill in the centers.

Color Illustration, page 30

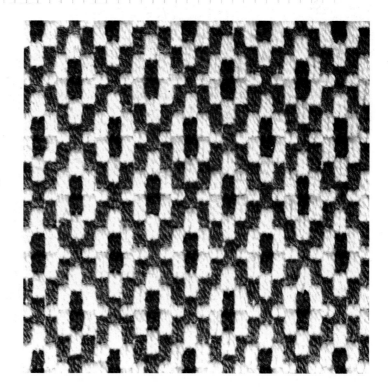

page 28

page 33

page 29

page 34

page 32

page 35

page 36

page 37

page 38

page 39

page 40

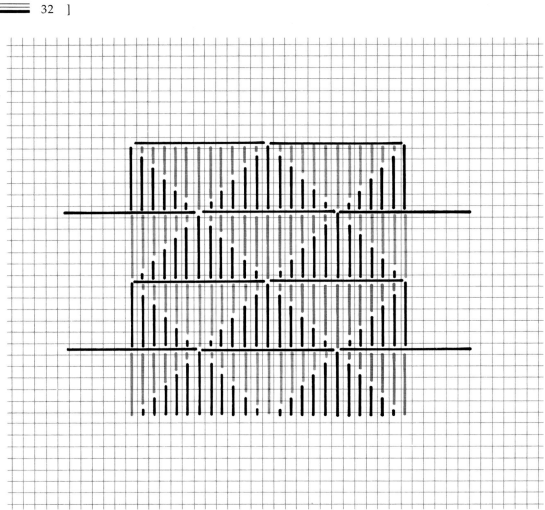

#12 Canvas
4-ply Tapestry Yarn
4 Colors

This easy pattern works up very fast. Work the pattern diagonally, one shade at a time, so that you don't have to switch threads constantly. The horizontal stitch is done at the end, one color at a time, on top of the work.

Color Illustration, page 30

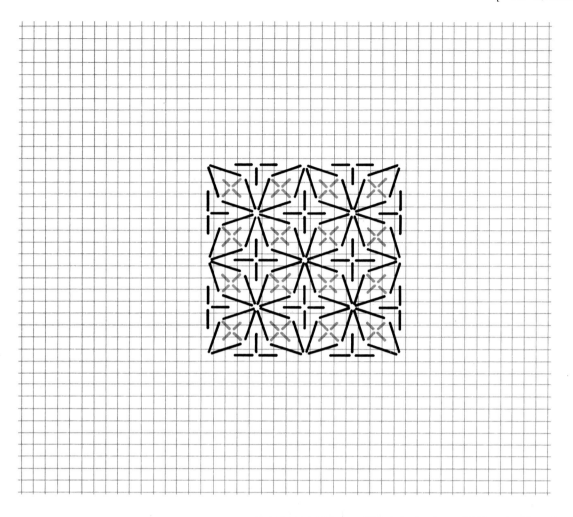

#5 Canvas
Quickpoint Yarn
3 Colors

This pattern consists of
three different-sized
stars. Work one size at a
time in diagonal rows.
Note that the smallest
star is tilted in a different
direction than the others.

Color Illustration, page 30

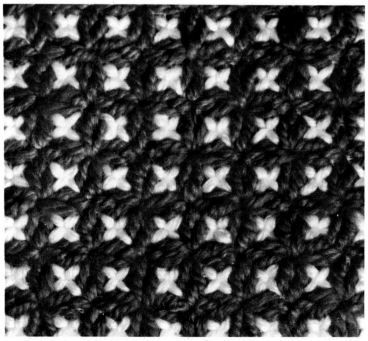

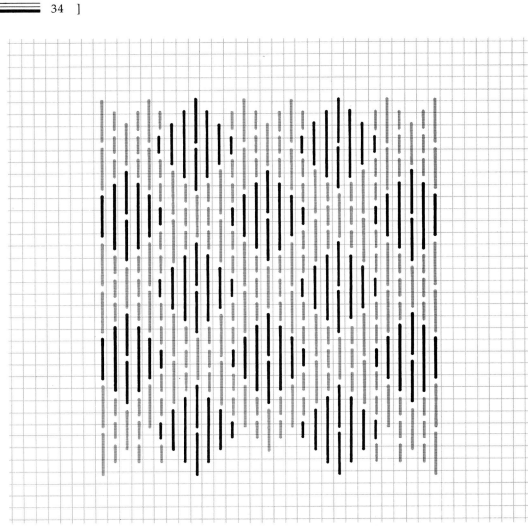

#10 Canvas
3-ply Persian-type Yarn
3 Colors

This is a complicated
one. First work the
diamonds in diagonal
rows. Then fill in the
background, alternating
one long stitch and two
short stitches.

Color Illustration, page 30

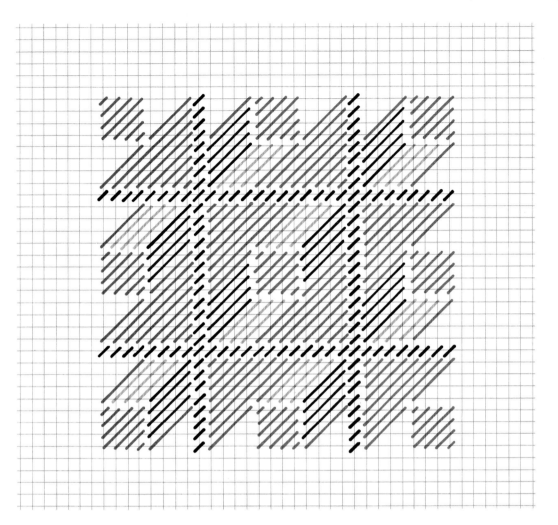

#10 Canvas
4-ply Tapestry Yarn
4 Colors

A very clean design,
worked with four
needles, one for each
color. Complete one large
square at a time, starting
each with the small
center square.

Color Illustration, page 30

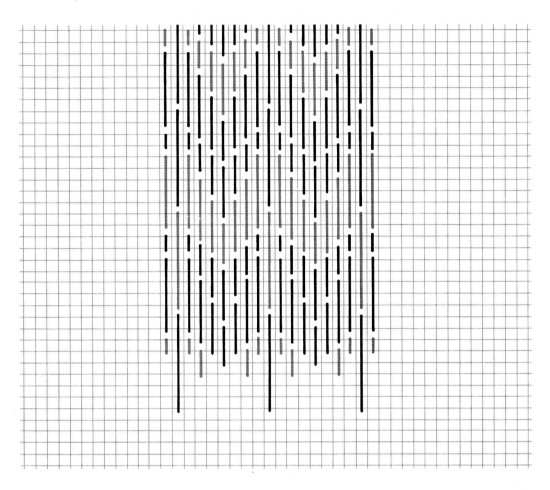

#10 Canvas
3-ply Persian-type Yarn
3 Colors

Here is a slightly unusual
Bargello pattern. As in all
Bargello, establish one
horizontal line first and
the others will fall into
place.

Color Illustration, page 31

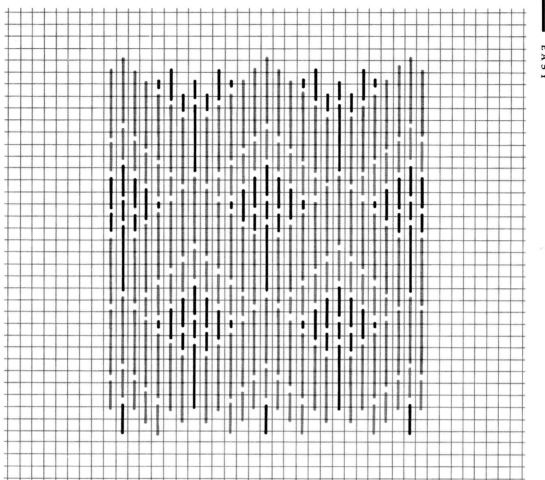

#10 Canvas
3-ply Persian-type Yarn
4 Colors

A very handsome
pattern, quick to work.
Begin with the horizontal
zigzag line of the
background. Then fill in
the little "trees."

Color Illustration, page 31

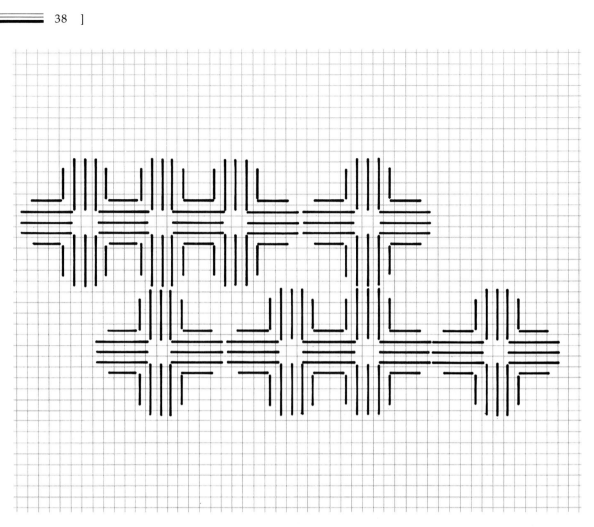

#10 Canvas
3-ply Persian-type Yarn
4 Colors

A pretty floral pattern
with irregular clusters of
flowers. Working with
two needles, first do the
flowers with straight
stitches in horizontal
rows across the canvas.
Fill in the centers of the
flowers with French
knots or cross-stitches,
and then do the
background in the
continental or basket-
weave stitch.

Color Illustration, page 31

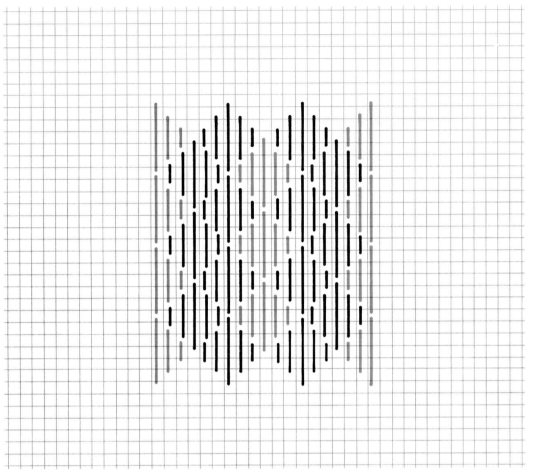

**#10 Canvas
3-ply Persian-type Yarn
3 Colors**

Work the diamonds in vertical rows, one color at a time. This pattern would make a lovely belt or a headband because the design is in such compact rows.

Color Illustration, page 31

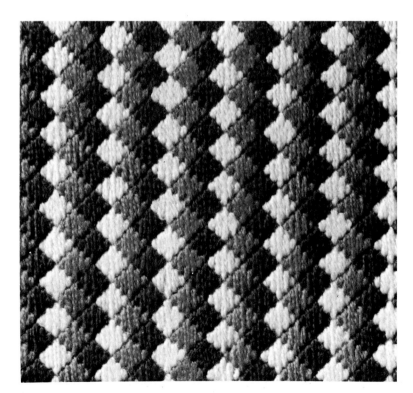

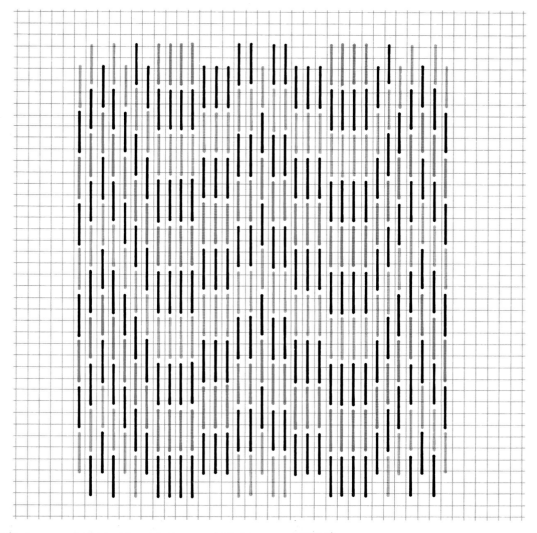

**#10 Canvas
3-ply Persian-type Yarn
4 Colors**

Another very typical
Bargello pattern. It is
best to establish one
horizontal line first.

Color Illustration, page 31

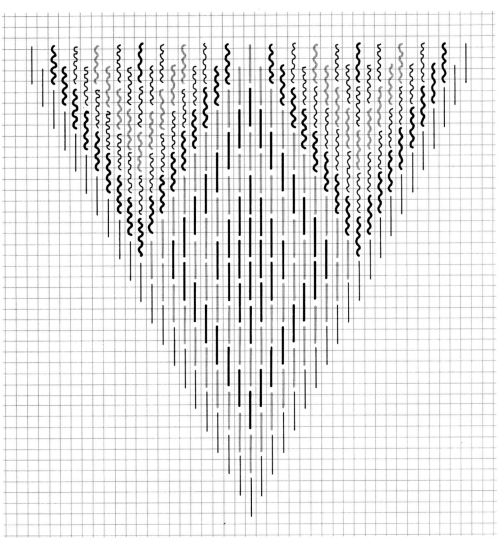

#12 Canvas
4-ply Tapestry Yarn
8 Colors

This pattern consists of
the outline of a large
diamond, which is filled
with four smaller
diamonds. Of course,
these smaller diamonds
are themselves formed by
concentric lines going
toward the tiny diamond
at each center. Note that
the chart shows only half
of one large diamond. To
continue, work in
a mirror image.

Color Illustration, page 50

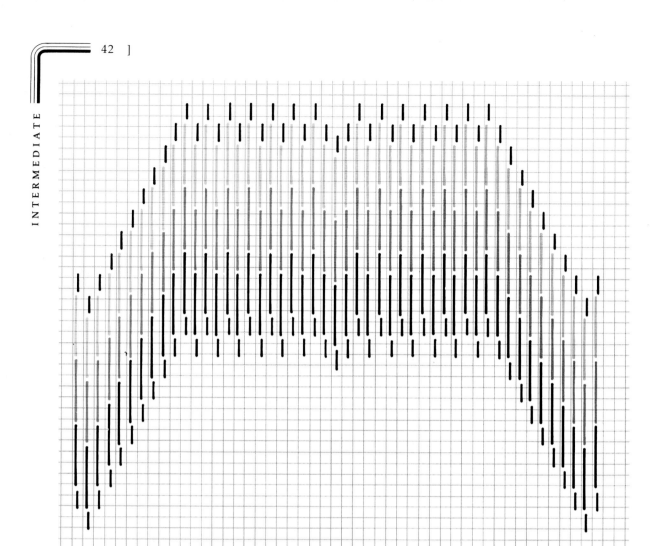

**#12 Canvas
3-ply Persian-type Yarn
4 Colors**

A contemporary,
dramatic Bargello pattern,
following extreme peaks.
Though this looks
complicated, it is actually
an easy pattern to work.
Work horizontally, one
color at a time.

Color Illustration, page 50

#12 Canvas
3-ply Persian-type Yarn
3 Colors

Establish the diagonal
lines across the canvas.
Then fill in each
diamond, one at a time,
working with two
needles. Keep an even
tension, especially on
the long stitches.

Color Illustration, page 50

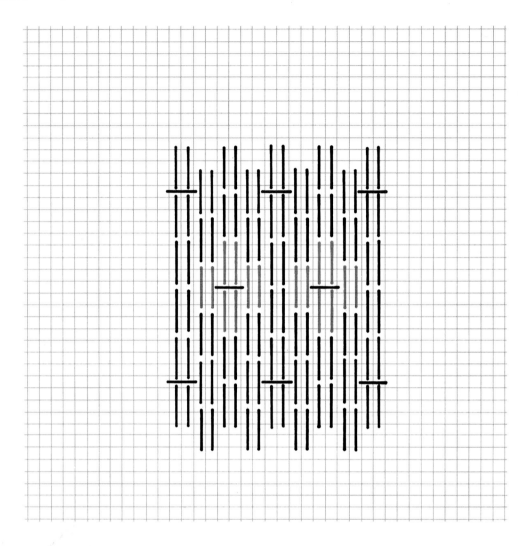

#12 Canvas
4-ply Tapestry Yarn
3 Colors

This is a lovely, delicate design in these nostalgic colors. It is very easy. Establish the horizontal line across the canvas and the other colors will follow. The centers of the flowers are in alternating rows of color. Lay these in like a small running stitch.

Color Illustration, page 50

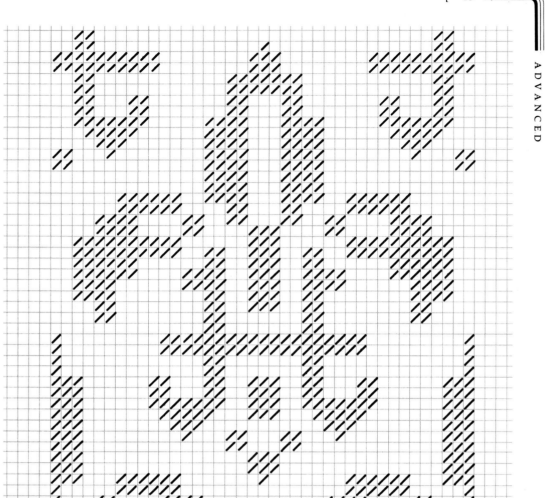

#10 Canvas
3-ply Persian-type Yarn
2 Colors

A pretty fleur-de-lis
pattern on which you
have to concentrate
carefully. Follow the
chart, counting
accurately, to establish
one fleur-de-lis at a time.
Then fill in the
background in a
contrasting color. Use
either the continental or
basket-weave stitch for
this design.

/ = white
blue background

Color Illustration, page 50

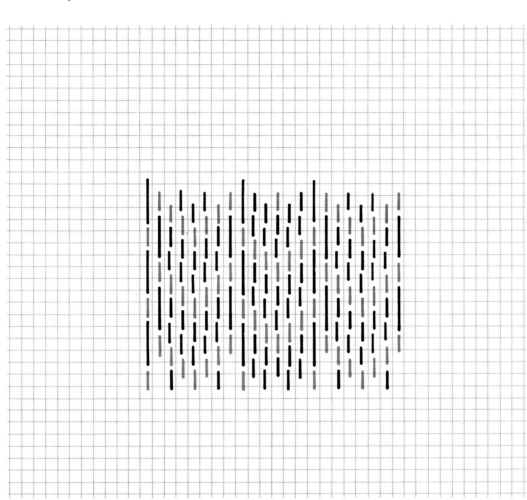

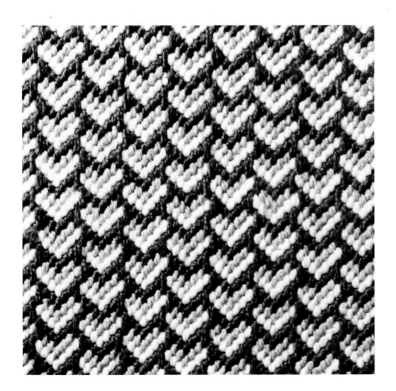

#10 Canvas
3-ply Persian-type Yarn
3 Colors

This pattern is very good
for small objects. Note
that it consists of two
small V's set in a frame-
work. Work the frame
first, then fill in the
other colors.

Color Illustration, page 51

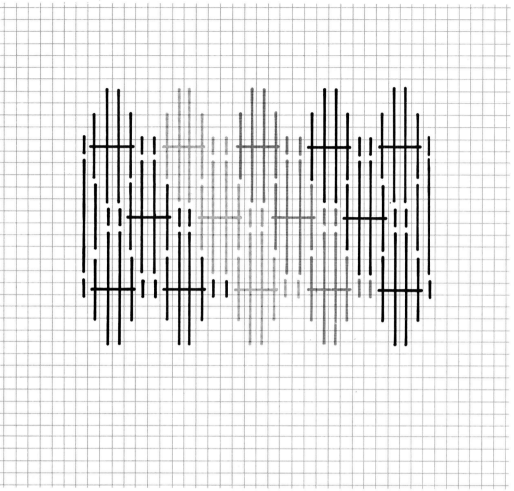

#12 Canvas
4-ply Tapestry Yarn
4 Colors

In these colors, this is a
very soft, romantic
pattern. Work diagonally,
one color at a time. The
horizontal bars go *on top*
of the work and can be
done after everything
else is finished.

Color Illustration, page 51

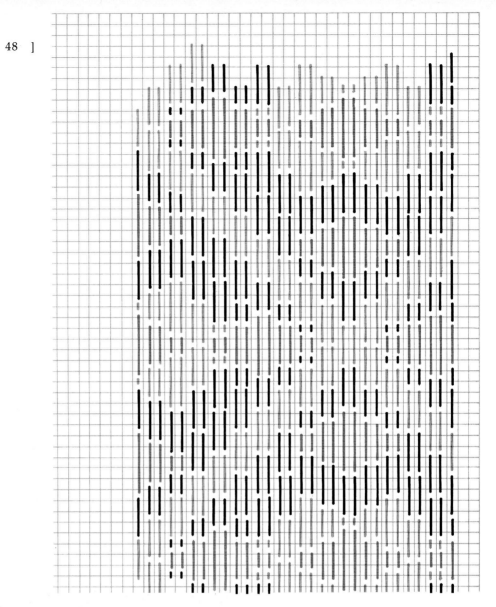

#12 Canvas
3-ply Persian-type Yarn
4 Colors

Another "framed-cloud" design that has a really pretty look. First establish the diagonal framework across the canvas. Then fill in the diamonds, one at a time, counting carefully. Note that the chart shows only half the repeat. To continue the pattern, work in a mirror image.

Color Illustration, page 51

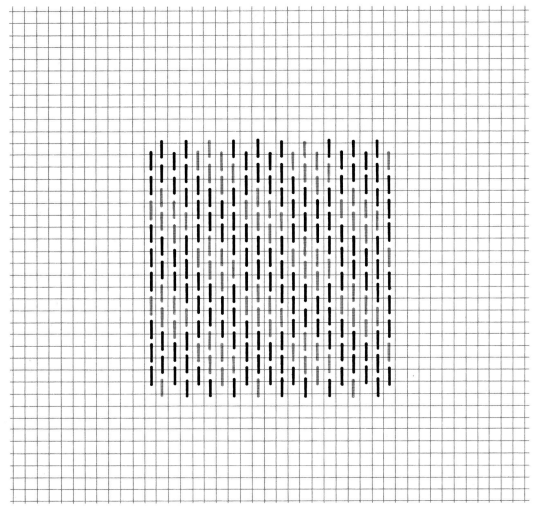

#5 Canvas
Quickpoint Yarn
4 Colors

Work the diagonal
lines first. Then fill in
the other colors, one at a
time. Like most quick-
point, this works up to a
very bold pattern on a
#5 canvas. If you like,
you can use a finer mesh
and a finer yarn and
come out with a more
delicate effect, suitable
for a smaller piece.

Color Illustration, page 51

page 43

page 41

page 44

page 42

page 45

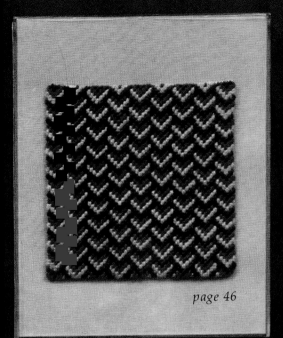

page 46

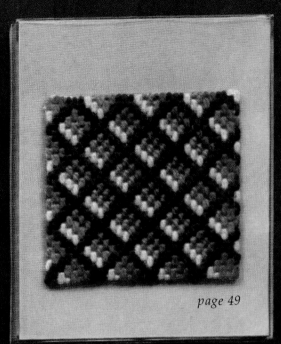

page 49

page 47

page 52

page 48

page 53

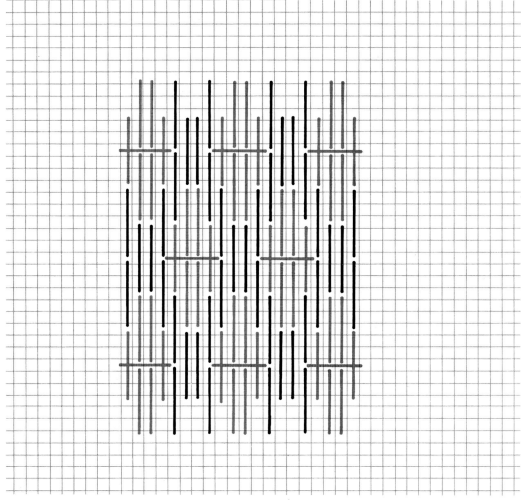

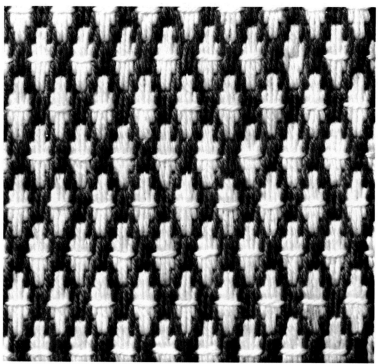

#12 Canvas
4-ply Tapestry Yarn
3 Colors

First work the zigzagging
vertical lines. Then fill
in the centers. Note that
the stitches in the center
are broken in half, and to
cover this, they are
overlapped with a
straight horizontal
stitch right on top of the
work.

Color Illustration, page 51

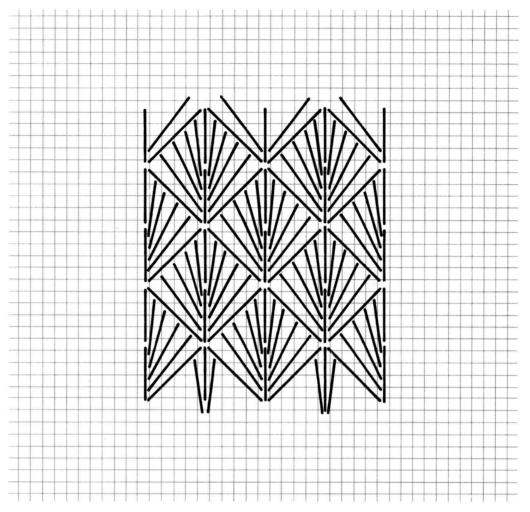

#5 Canvas
Quickpoint Yarn
2 Colors

A lovely, leafy-looking design that does require careful counting. The difficulty is that you have to count the canvas threads diagonally, but once you have done a few leaves, you'll find it easy. The straight stitch in each leaf lays on top of the work.

Color Illustration, page 51

ADVANCED

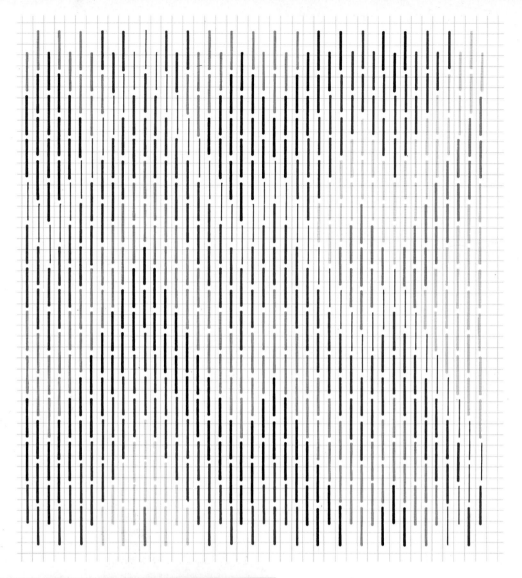

#12 Canvas
3-ply Persian-type Yarn
8 Colors

This is a very dramatic
Bargello pattern. Contrary
to the way I usually
tackle Bargello, the
easiest way to work this
design is to establish the
white framework first.
Then fill in, shade by
shade, working across
the canvas. Note that the
chart shows only half the
motif. To continue the
pattern, work in a mirror
image.

page 56

page 57

page 60

page 61

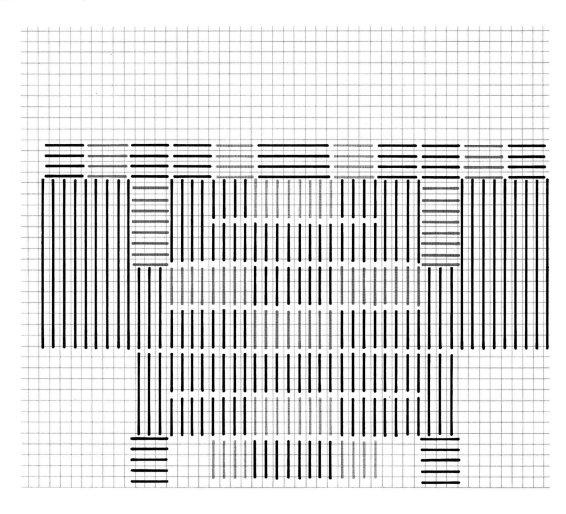

**#12 Canvas
3-ply Persian-type Yarn
4 Colors**

Another primitive-
looking pattern that is
complicated only because
the color changes very
often, requiring a bit of
concentration. A good
place to start is in the
center box. Note that the
chart shows little more
than half the repeat. To
continue, work in a
mirror image.

Color Illustration, page 55

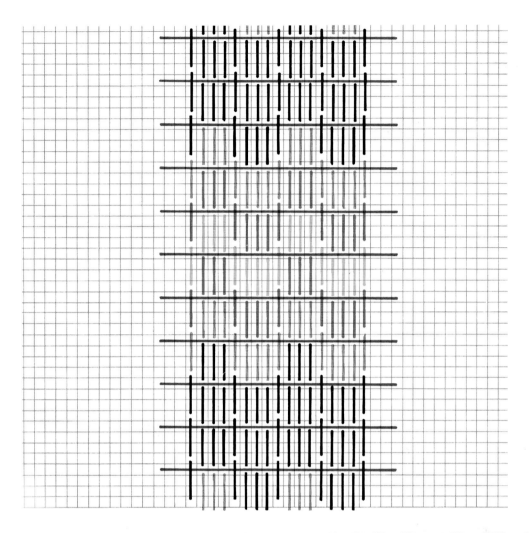

#12 Canvas
4-ply Tapestry Yarn
6 Colors

Each horizontal row is made up of two colors. Work with two needles straight across the canvas, establishing one row at a time. The running stitch, in another color, is in a pattern of "over three, under one, over three, under one" in horizontal lines.

Color Illustration, page 55

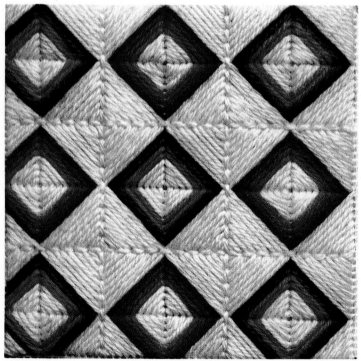

#10 Canvas
4-ply Tapestry Yarn
8 Colors

Form the colored
diamonds first. Then fill
in the background. Next
outline, with a running
stitch on top of the work,
each of the squares you
have formed.

**#12 Canvas
4-ply Tapestry Yarn
9 Colors**

With its stained-glass
look, this is one of my
favorite patterns. Work
across the canvas, one
color at a time. Note that
the white line separates
the two groups of colors.

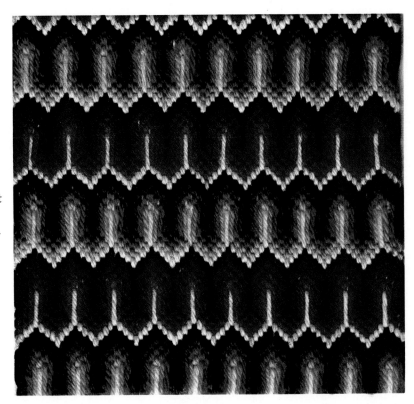

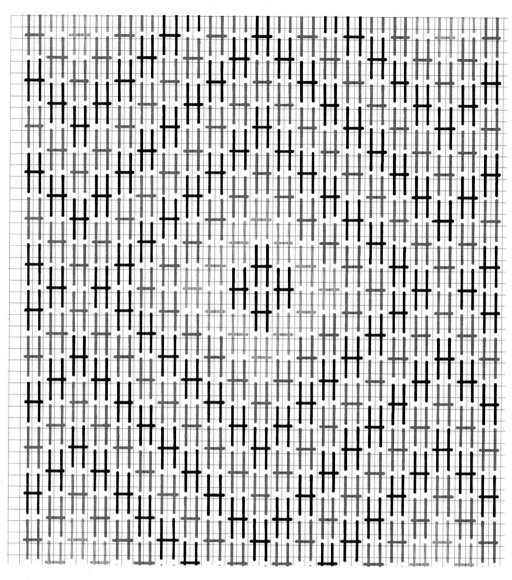

#12 Canvas
3-ply Persian-type Yarn
4 Colors

This pattern is done with
an H-shaped stitch. Work
one color at a time across
the canvas, as in any
Bargello pattern.

Color Illustration, page 55

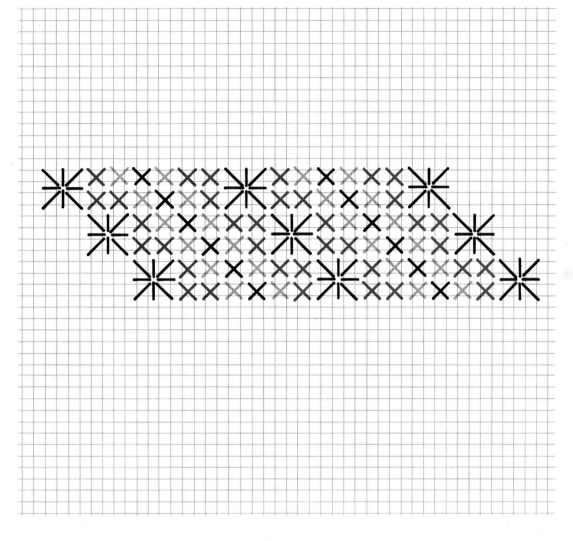

#10 Canvas
3-ply Persian-type Yarn
4 Colors

This is a cross-stitch
pattern. Work diagonally,
one color at a time. The
cross-stitch that covers
four canvas threads has
an upright cross in its
center.

Color Illustration, page 55

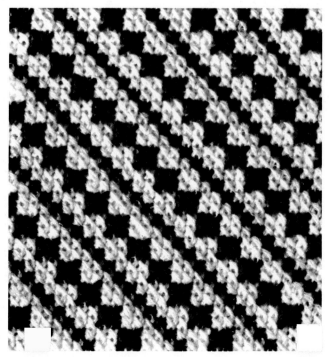

▰ = dark green
● = yellow
╱ = light pink
✕ = fuchsia
■ = black
— = light green
• = white

#5 Canvas
Quickpoint Yarn
7 Colors

I've called this
uncomplicated
quickpoint pattern
"advanced" because of
the frequent changes of
color. Look at the design
as composed of
horizontal and vertical
bars of three colors each.
Work the horizontal bars
first, then the vertical. In
the end, fill in the single
corner stitch that
separates the bars.

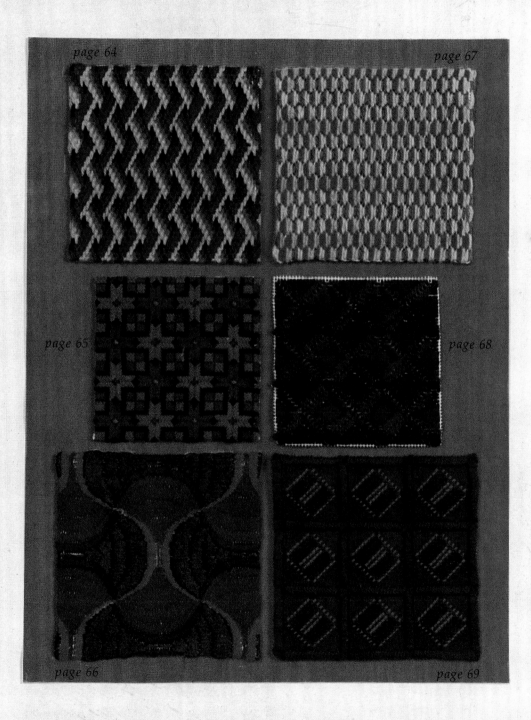

page 64

page 67

page 65

page 68

page 66

page 69

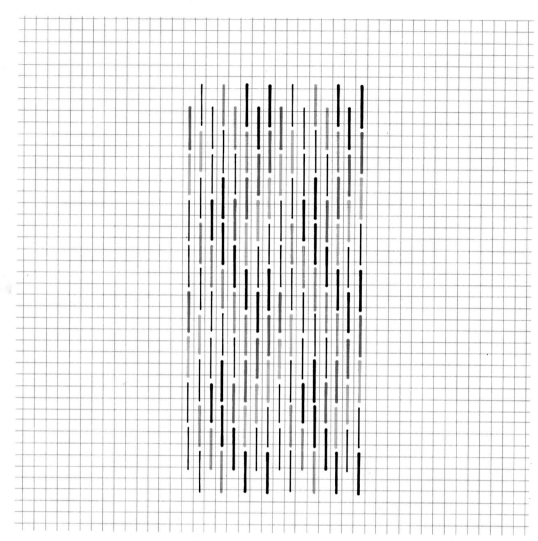

#12 Canvas
4-ply Tapestry Yarn
7 Colors

A Bargello pattern slightly different than usual because you do not establish a connected horizontal line. The pattern consists of two sets of slanted rectangles. Work one set of rectangles at a time, using three needles. Then work the rectangles slanting in the other direction. At the end, fill in the stitch between rectangles.

Color Illustration, page 63

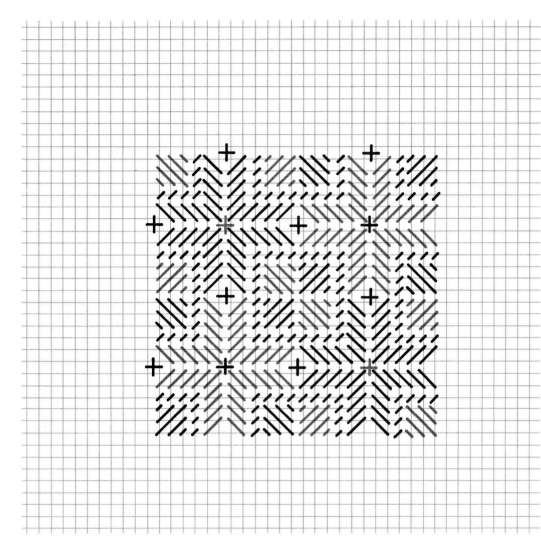

#10 Canvas
4-ply Tapestry Yarn
3 Colors

Start in the center of each
flower and work all the
flowers first. The position
of the boxes will then fall
in place automatically.
Don't be confused by the
cross-stitch at the center
of each flower. By
following the chart
carefully, you will see
that this is done on *top*
of the stitches and can be
filled in last.

Color Illustration, page 63

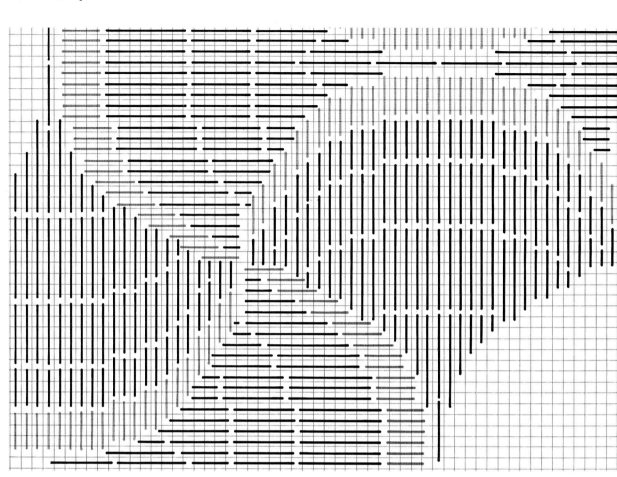

#12 Canvas
3-ply Persian-type Yarn
4 Colors

A beautiful, dramatic
pattern with a lot of
movement. Work one
"tree" at a time, taking
care, as usual, to pull the
threads with even
tension. You will note
from the photograph that
the "tree" is repeated
throughout, but in
different directions.

Color Illustration, page 63

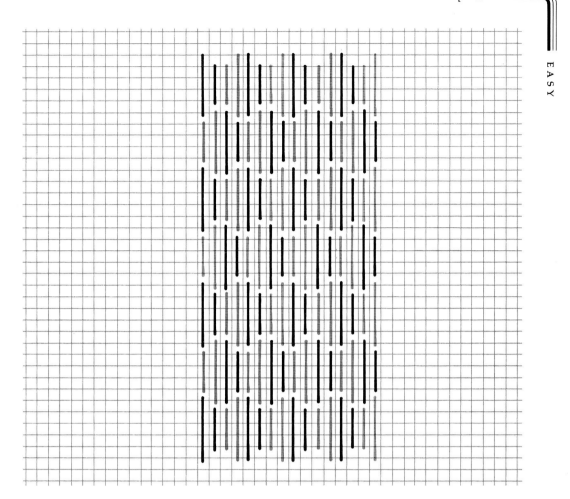

#12 Canvas
4-ply Tapestry Yarn
4 Colors

This is a quite busy
pattern that lends itself,
for example, to an
eyeglass case or other
small object. Think of the
pattern as rows of four-
petaled creatures and
work one horizontal row
at a time.

Color Illustration, page 63

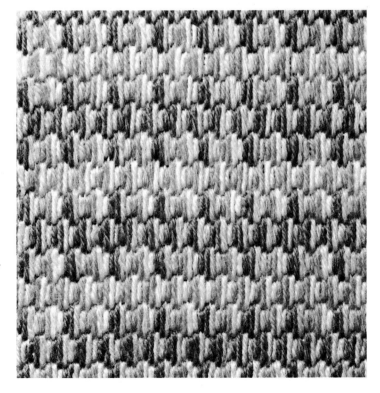

ADVANCED

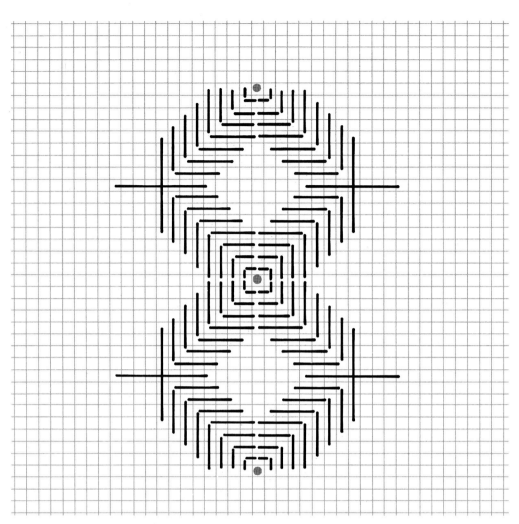

#10 Canvas
4-ply Tapestry Yarn
3 Colors

In the red and green I've
worked this pattern, it
has a lovely Christmas
look. The leaves are done
in straight stitches set
against a basket-weave or
continental background.
Work one color at a time,
diagonally, leaving a
space at every other
intersection for a French
knot (see chart). Then fill
in the background in
basket-weave or
continental.

Color Illustration, page 63

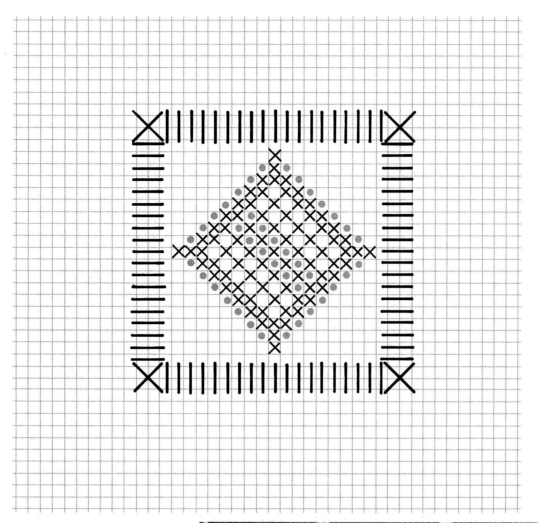

#10 Canvas
3-ply Persian-type Yarn
3 Colors

Establish the vertical and horizontal frames with straight stitches. Then do the cross-stitches at the corners. Finally, fill in one square at a time, using the continental or basket-weave stitch.

  ✕ = green
  ● = yellow
red background

Color Illustration, page 63

▲ = black
• = green
● = orange
✕ = brown
∨ = yellow
╱ = tan

#10 Canvas
4-ply Tapestry Yarn
6 Colors

A plaid design in the
continental or basket-
weave stitch. Establish
the single diagonal lines
in the continental stitch.
You will now have
outlined squares in a
diagonal fashion. Work
one square at a time,
doing the corner boxes
first in 4 colors in the
continental or basket-
weave stitch. Finally, fill
in the x-shaped back-
grounds of each square.

Color Illustration, page 82

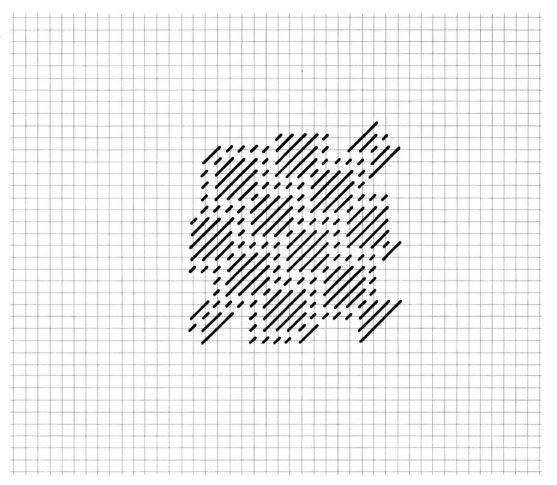

#10 Canvas
3-ply Persian-type Yarn
2 Colors

Work the continental
diagonal lines first. Then
the squares will fall in
automatically.

Color Illustration, page 82

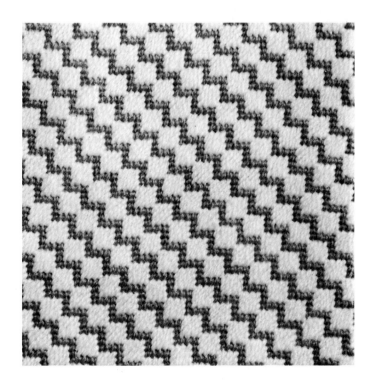

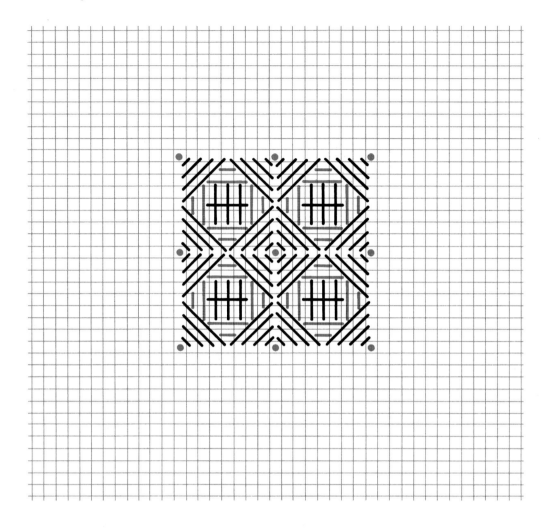

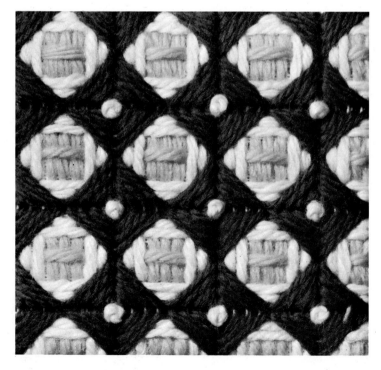

#5 Canvas
Quickpoint Yarn
3 Colors

Establish the diamonds first. Then fill in the centers. The horizontal lines in the centers of alternate diamonds are on top of existing stitches. Add the French knots at the end.

Color Illustration, page 82

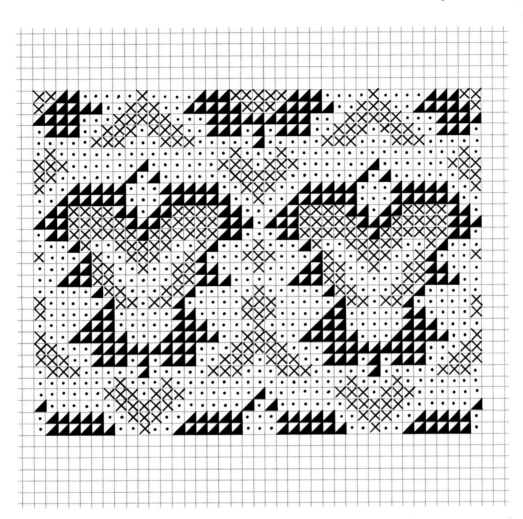

▲ = black
• = white
✕ = green

#12 Canvas
4-ply Tapestry Yarn
3 Colors

In the continental or
basket-weave stitch,
this pattern has a
traditional heraldic effect.
(You could, if you're
feeling very elegant, put
your own initials in the
center of one of the
shields.) Work one shield
at a time and then fill in
the background, working
with two needles.

Color Illustration, page 82

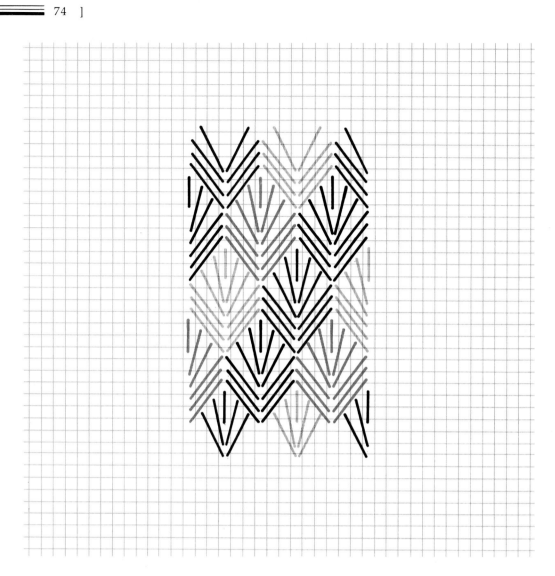

#5 Canvas
Quickpoint Yarn
4 Colors

Another lovely, leafy design which is difficult only because you must count the lines of the leaf diagonally.

Color Illustration, page 82

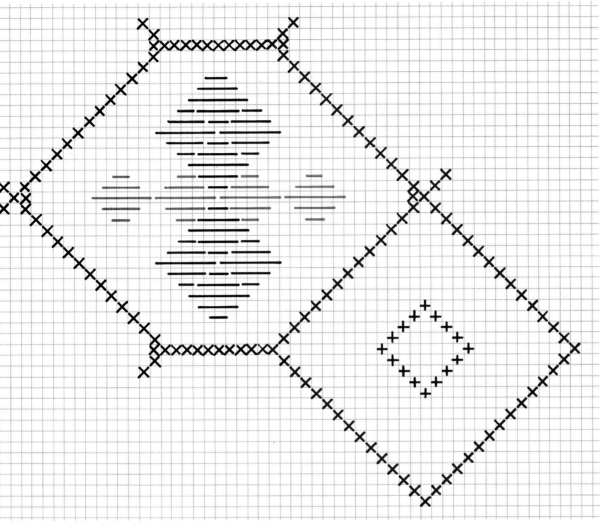

#10 Canvas
3-ply Persian-type Yarn
3 Colors (plus background)

This pattern contains
straight stitches with the
basket-weave or
continental as
background. It consists of
two differently shaped
diamonds. Establish one
complete row of
diamonds horizontally
across the canvas. Then
the remaining row of
diamonds will fall into
place.

Color Illustration, page 82

#12 Canvas
4-ply Tapestry Yarn
4 Colors

Work one diamond at a
time, starting with the
center diamond. Fill in
the cross-stitches at
the end.

Color Illustration, page 83

E A S Y

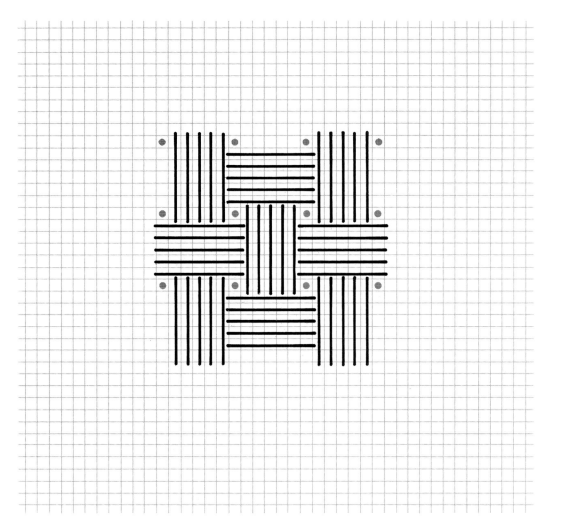

**#12 Canvas
4-ply Tapestry Yarn
3 Colors**

A clean, delicate pattern
that is very easy. Work
one color at a time, one
box at a time, in any
direction you like. The
French knots are added
at the end, with the yarn
twisted only once around
the needle.

Color Illustration, page 83

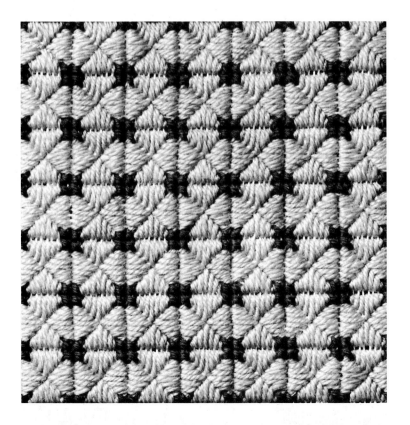

#12 Canvas
4-ply Tapestry Yarn
2 Colors

This is one of those patterns that is very easy to do and very hard to explain. One look at the chart and the photograph and you'll be on your way.

Color Illustration, page 83

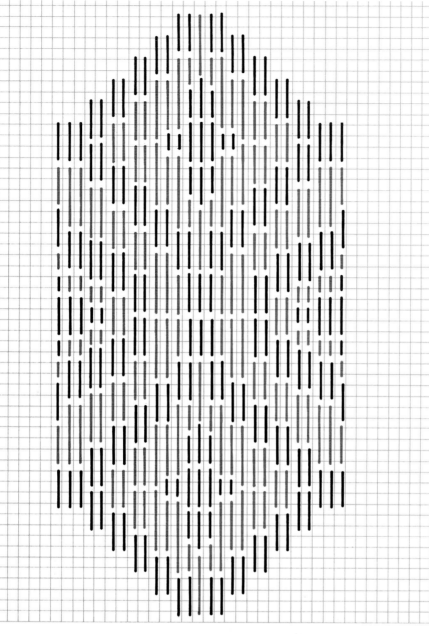

#12 Canvas
3-ply Persian-type Yarn
3 Colors

If you are ready for
another challenge, this is
a tough one because no
thread is carried all the
way across the canvas.
The way I work it is to
establish all the
connecting diamonds
over the entire work, and
then the centers fall into
place. To move from the
repeat shown here, work
in a mirror image.

Color Illustration, page 83

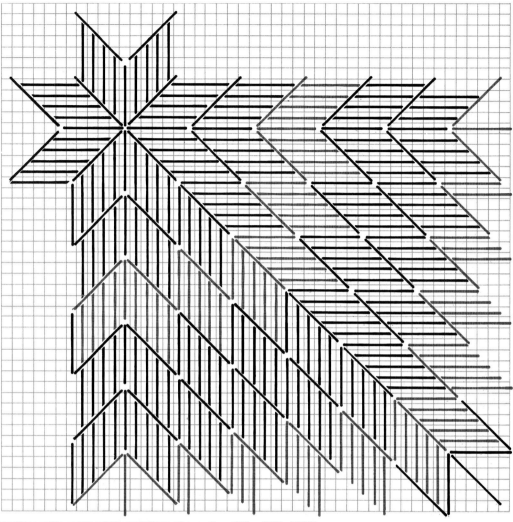

#10 Canvas
3-ply Persian-type Yarn
3 Colors

Start in the center, working one color at a time in concentric circles, keeping a very accurate count. The straight diagonal stitches are put on top of the work. This pattern is like a sunburst and can be extended to any size, depending on what you're making. To continue pattern, work in a mirror image.

Color Illustration, page 83

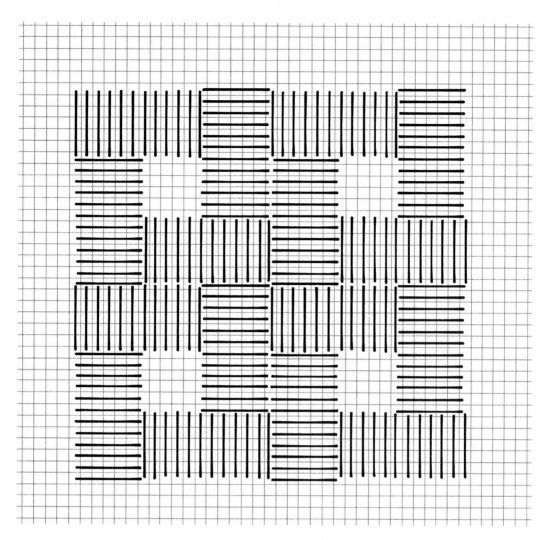

#10 Canvas
3-ply Persian-type Yarn
2 Colors

A very easy, satisfying arrangement of boxes in alternating colors. Work one square at a time, pulling the yarn with an even tension. Fill in the center of each box with French knots or cross-stitches

Color Illustration, page 83

page 70

page 71

page 72

page 73

page 74

page 75

page 76

page 77

page 78

page 79

page 80

page 81

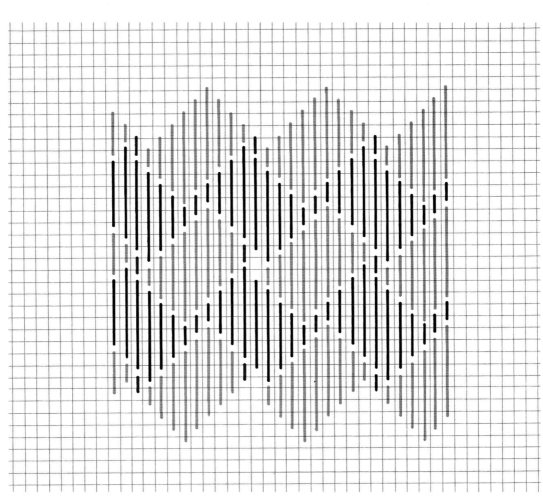

#5 Canvas
Quickpoint Yarn
3 Colors

Another lovely, easy
pattern with a quilted
effect. Work one little
"cushion" at a time. Fill
in straight little corner
stitches at the end.

Color Illustration, page 86

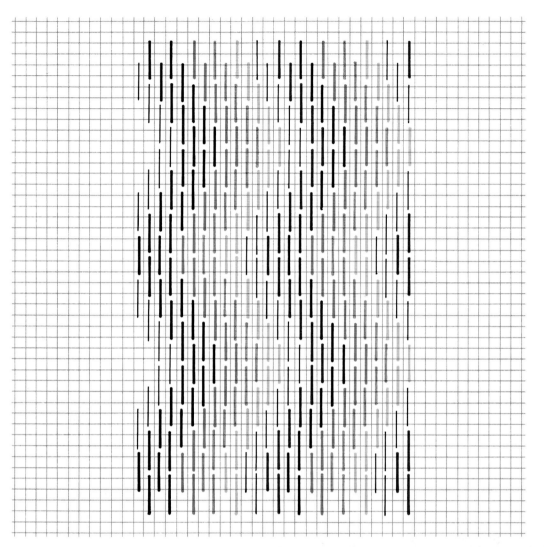

#12 Canvas
4-ply Tapestry Yarn
6 Colors

A Bargello pattern which
you can use in the
direction shown or
turned horizontally.
Establish the continuous
lines across the canvas
first and then fill in the
centers, which consist
of four different shades.

Color Illustration, page 86

page 84

page 88

page 85

page 89

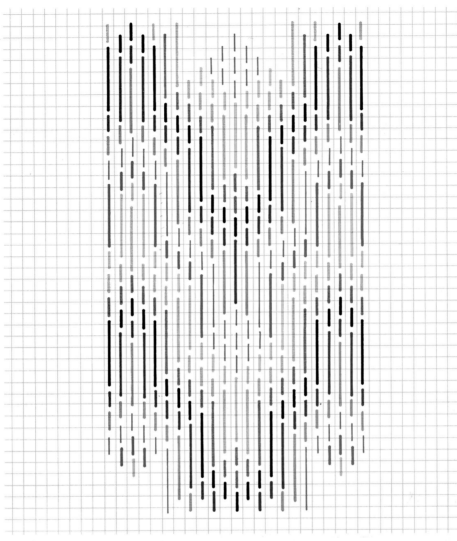

#10 Canvas
4-ply Tapestry Yarn
8 Colors

A very interesting
Bargello pattern. Work
one shade at a time
horizontally and this
pattern will fall quickly
into place.

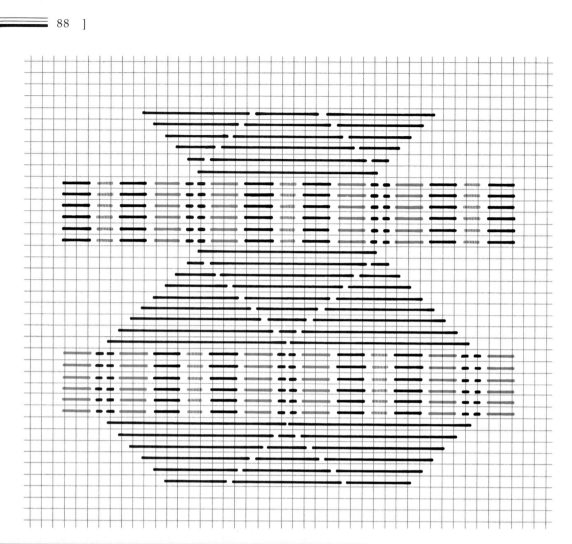

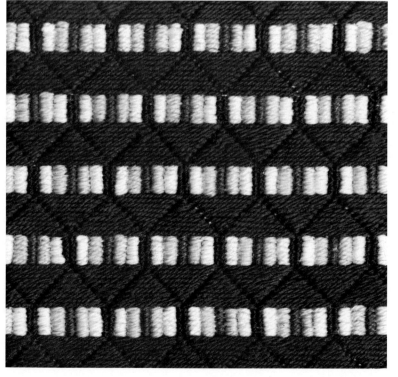

#12 Canvas
4-ply Tapestry Yarn
4 Colors

This is a charming pattern. Work one diamond shape at a time, including the center colors. You'll find it easier to work with four needles.

Color Illustration, page 86

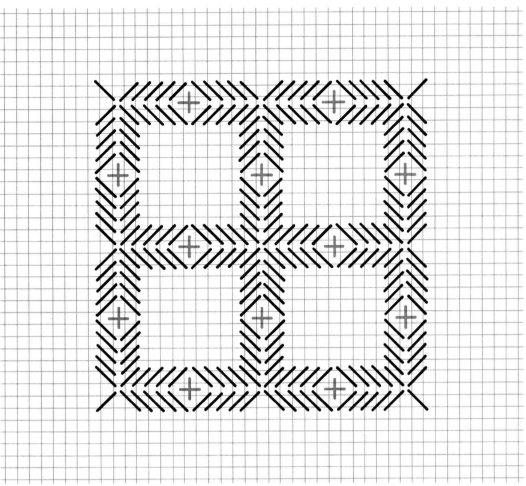

#10 Canvas
3-ply Persian-type Yarn
3 Colors

This is a very regular, bright-looking pattern. Do the crosses first, in one color, vertically and horizontally across the canvas. Between each cross there is a small diamond, with a cross-stitch at its center. To finish the piece, fill in the background with the continental or basket-weave stitch.

Color Illustration, page 86

#12 Canvas
4-ply Tapestry Yarn
9 Colors

This lovely pattern is like
an embroidered
kaleidoscope. If you look
carefully, you'll notice
that the beige wool forms
a diagonal framework.
Do the beige first, then
fill in the diamonds, one
color at a time, starting at
the center of each
diamond. Though it
looks as if they don't,
these straight stitches all
go in the same direction.

page 92

page 96

page 93

page 97

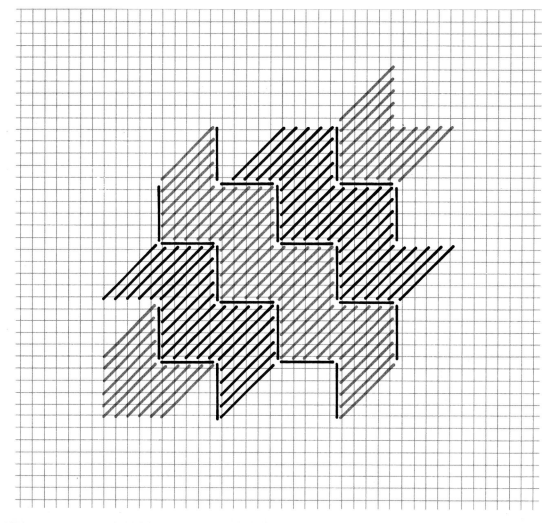

#10 Canvas
3-ply Persian-type Yarn
3 Colors

This is a variation of the
internationally known
Byzantine stitch. As in all
Byzantine-type patterns,
watch out for the corners.
Follow the chart carefully.
Use a straight stitch to
make the outline.

Color Illustration, page 91

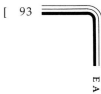

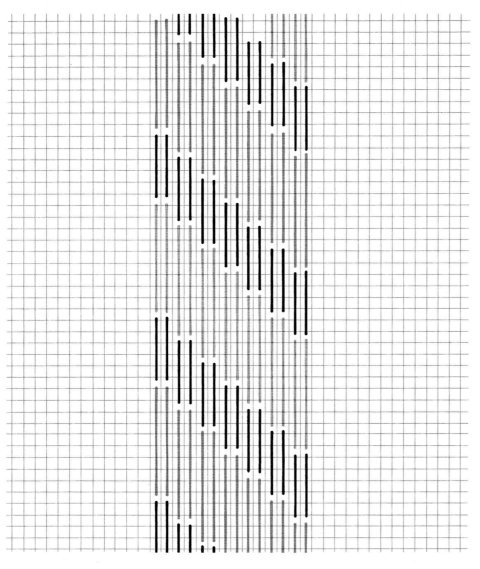

**#12 Canvas
3-ply Persian-type Yarn
4 Colors**

A perfect pattern for a
beginner because it is so
easy and clear. Work one
diagonal row at a time.

Color Illustration, page 91

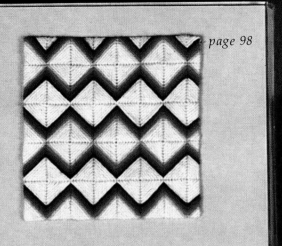

page 98

page 99

page 101

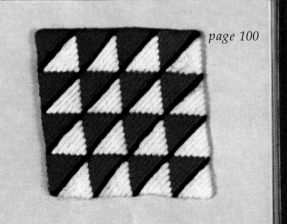

page 100

page 102

page 103

page 105

page 104

page 106

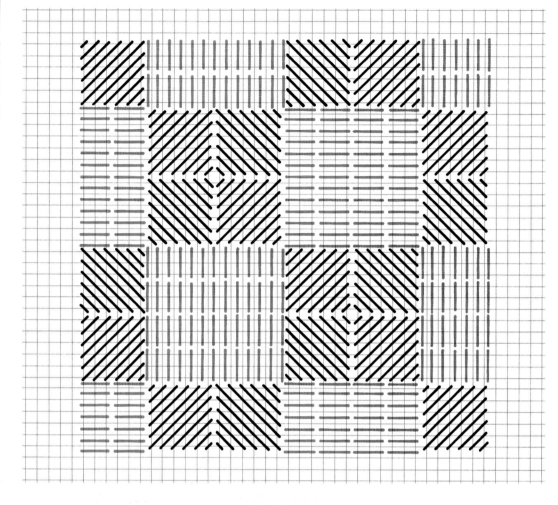

**#10 Canvas
4-ply Tapestry Yarn
3 Colors**

Establish the checkerboards first (note the change of direction of the checkers). Then work the bars between, in horizontal and vertical directions.

Color Illustration, page 91

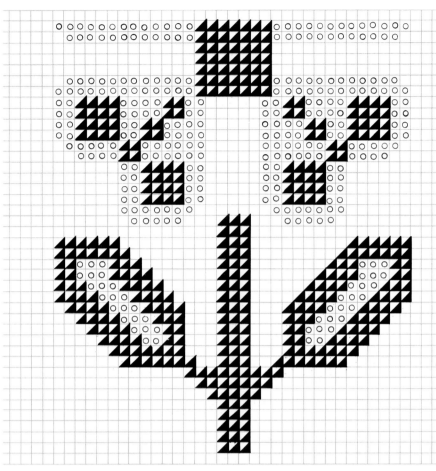

▲ = blue
○ = orange
white background

#10 Canvas
3-ply Persian-type Yarn
2 Colors (plus background)

This traditional flower
done in the continental
or basket-weave stitch
can be placed wherever
you like on the canvas
and repeated as often as
you like. Note that only
half the flower is shown.
To continue, work in a
mirror image. The
background is done in
the basket-weave stitch.

Color Illustration, page 91

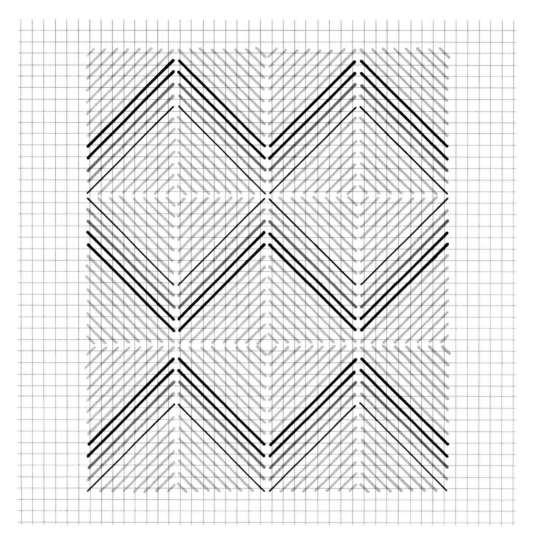

#10 Canvas
4-ply Tapestry Yarn
6 Colors

Look at this modern pattern as if it were made up of rectangular sections. Work each rectangle as a unit, using as many color changes as you prefer.

Color Illustration, page 94

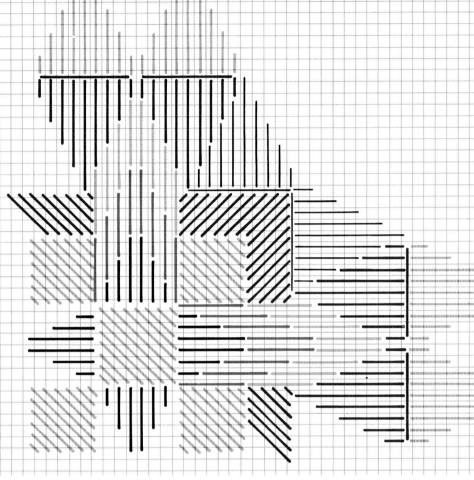

#12 Canvas
4-ply Tapestry Yarn
6 Colors (plus background)

An Indian-style design
that can be repeated, this
pattern also works well
centered on your piece.
Set it on a background of
the continental or basket-
weave stitch in a
contrasting color. Work
in quickpoint yarn on a
#5 canvas if you want
the design to be larger.
Note that the chart shows
little more than half the
motif. To continue the
pattern, work in a mirror
image.

Color Illustration, page 94

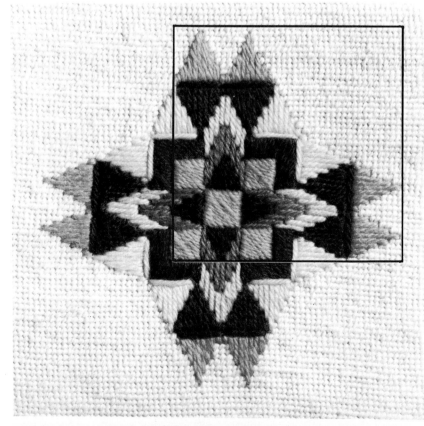

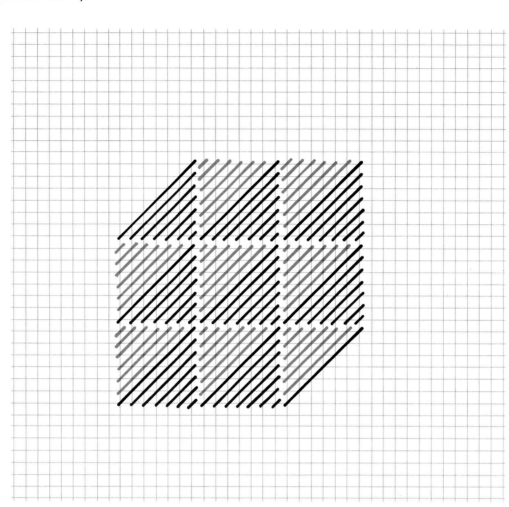

**#5 Canvas
Quickpoint Yarn
3 Colors**

An extremely easy,
attractive pattern, perfect
for a beginner. Work one
sail at a time, finishing
with the "dividing line"
in a contrasting color.

Color Illustration, page 94

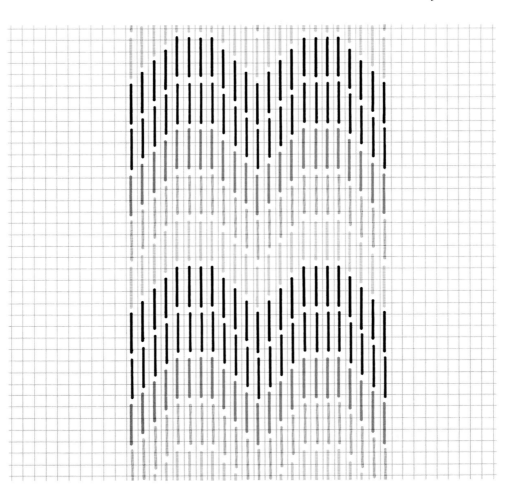

#10 Canvas
3-ply Persian-type Yarn
5 Colors

A very easy Bargello
pattern that would be
suitable for almost any
project, from an eyeglass
case to a chair seat.
Establish one horizontal
row first and the others
will fall into place.

Color Illustration, page 94

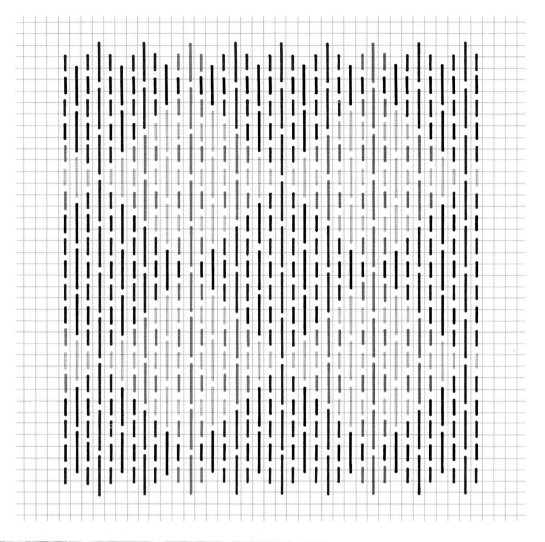

#12 Canvas
3-ply Persian-type Yarn
4 Colors

This one is challenging
because it is so busy. It
consists of tiny diamonds
made up of one long
stitch and two short.
These then become part
of a larger diamond.
Work each of these larger
diamond groups at a
time, alternating the
arrangement of colors.

Color Illustration, page 94

#10 Canvas
3-ply Persian-type Yarn
5 Colors

Save this pattern for a
piece large enough to
show its dramatic effect.
Work one color at a time
in the diagonal rows. Be
careful to count the
corners accurately.

Color Illustration, page 95

■ = black
◣ = brown
✕ = red-brown
● = gold
V = yellow
• = white

#12 Canvas
4-ply Tapestry Yarn
6 Colors

Work horizontally across the canvas, one color at a time. This delicate grospoint design is wonderful for a small piece, perhaps an eyeglass case or pincushion.

Color Illustration, page 95

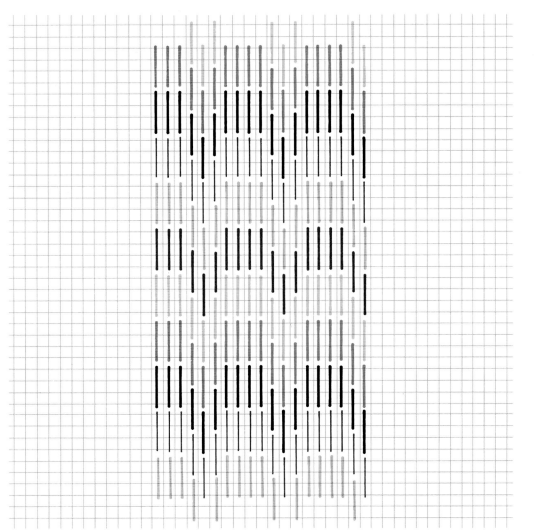

#12 Canvas
4-ply Tapestry Yarn
6 Colors

A typical Bargello
pattern, forming peaks.
Establish one horizontal
line first and the others
will follow easily.

Color Illustration, page 95

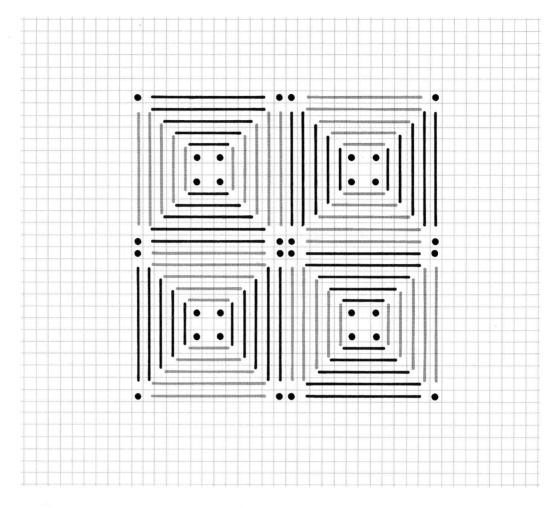

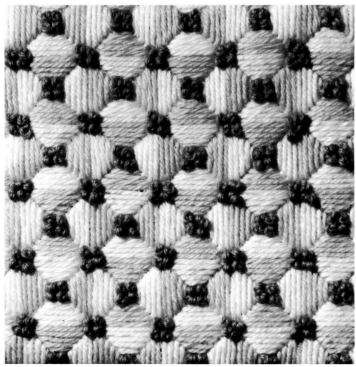

#10 Canvas
4-ply Tapestry Yarn
3 Colors

This lovely design is a
floral pattern in canvas
embroidery. You can, if
you like, use several
colors for the flowers.
Work with two needles at
a time. Do the French
knots at the end.

Color Illustration, page 95

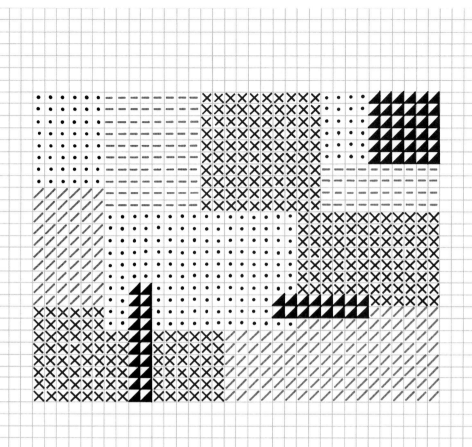

/ = light brown
◢ = dark brown
✕ = blue green
— = beige
• = white

#10 Canvas
3-ply Persian-type Yarn
5 Colors

At first glance this
pattern looks intricate
and irregular, like a very
complicated abstract
painting. However, when
you look at the chart
you'll see that by
working one color at a
time, the blocks of the
design will fall into place.
Count accurately though,
or you'll get into
difficulty.

Color Illustration, page 114

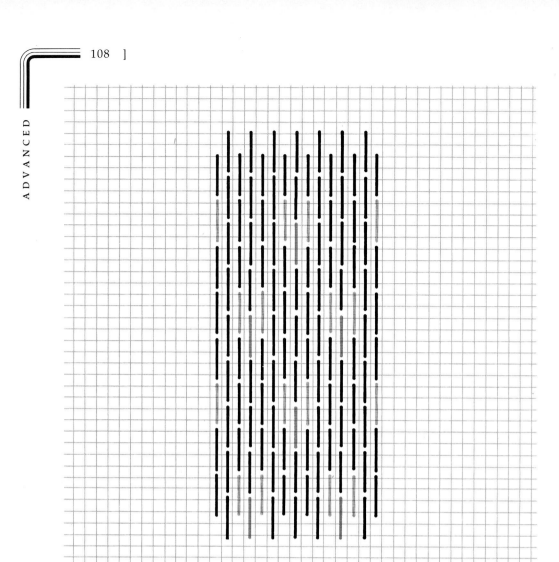

#12 Canvas
4-ply Tapestry Yarn
4 Colors

Although this pattern is
not very difficult, it *does*
require more counting than
most. You really do have to
count the centers first, moving
from one three-colored center
to the next in a *diagonal* line.
You will find, then, that
there are three canvas
threads between each yellow
stitch, between each red
stitch, etc., if you move in a
diagonal direction. This is
consistent throughout. After
the centers are complete, fill
in the background, still
continuing to work on
the diagonal.

Color Illustration, page 114

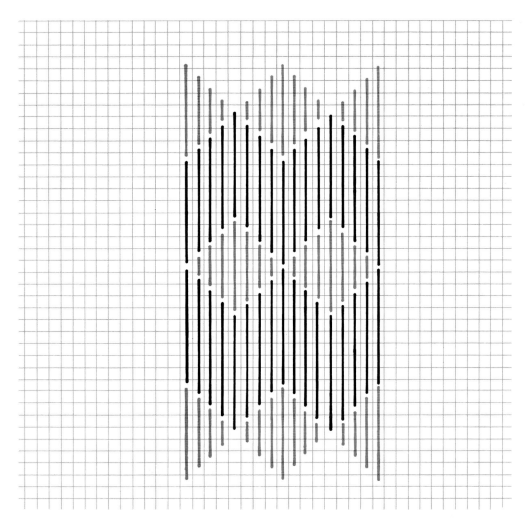

#10 Canvas
3-ply Persian-type Yarn
3 Colors

Work the diamonds across the canvas, leaving one space between each. When you work the gray and black, note that a black stitch always fills in this space between the diamonds.

Color Illustration, page 114

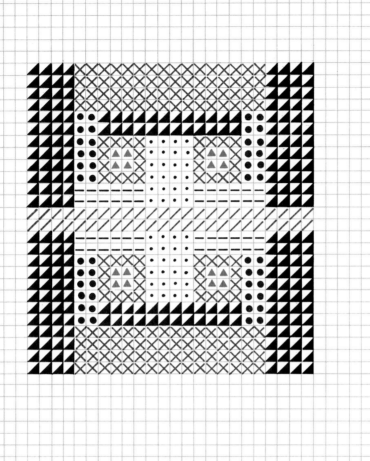

= black
• = white
● = green-blue
— = light orange
╱ = dark orange
✕ = light blue
▲ = yellow

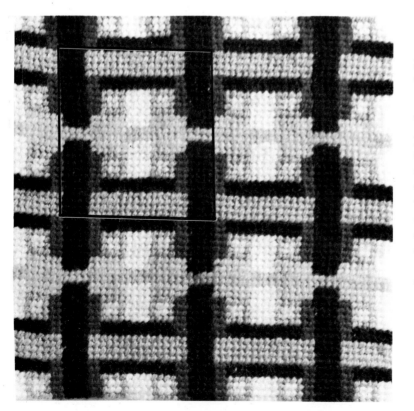

#10 Canvas
3-ply Persian-type Yarn
7 Colors

This cubist-looking pattern requires accurate counting and close attention. Use the continental or basket-weave stitch across the canvas and follow the chart exactly, working one full repeat at a time.

Color Illustration, page 114

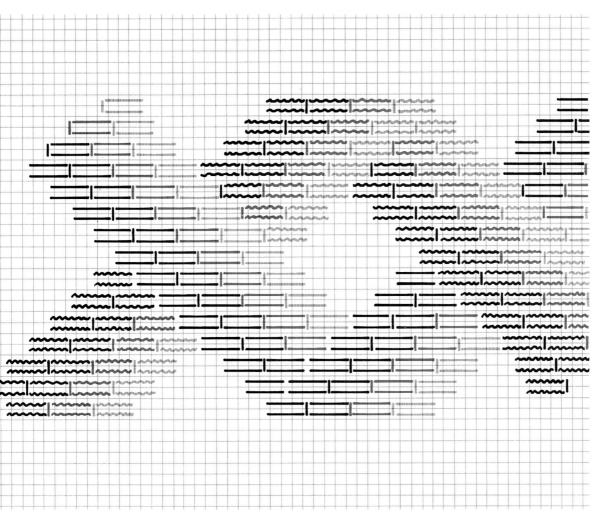

#12 Canvas
3-ply Persian-type Yarn
8 Colors (plus background)

This formal pattern could
be used for a belt if you
do only one chain. Each
zigzagging link of this
chain consists of four
colors. Work one
complete link at a time,
one color at a time, in a
straight stitch. I have
separated each shade in
the chain with a straight
vertical stitch, but you
can eliminate it if you
like. Work the background
in the continental
or basket-weave stitch.

Color Illustration, page 114

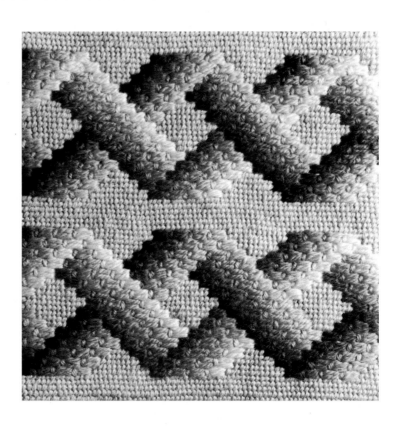

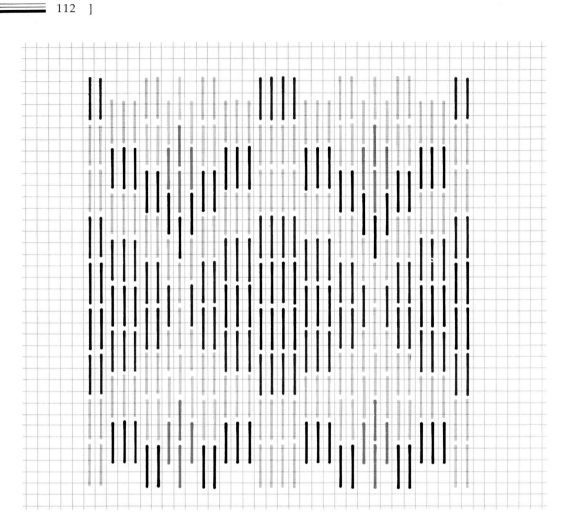

#10 Canvas
3-ply Persian-type Yarn
5 Colors

This is a typical Bargello
pattern, forming peaks
and curves. First work
across the canvas to
establish a horizontal
line. Then the other
shades will fall in place
easily.

Color Illustration, page 114

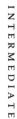

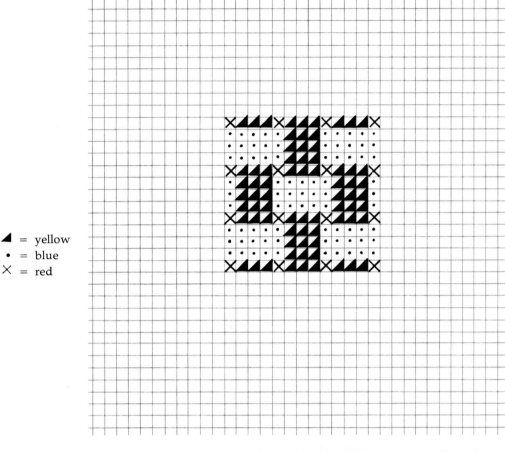

▲ = yellow
• = blue
✕ = red

#10 Canvas
3-ply Persian-type Yarn
3 Colors

Done in the continental
or basket-weave stitch,
this is a fairly easy
grospoint pattern that
requires careful counting.
Work with two needles,
completing one rectangle
at a time. Note that every
other rectangle changes
direction. Put in the
joining stitches in a
contrasting color at the
end.

Color Illustration, page 115

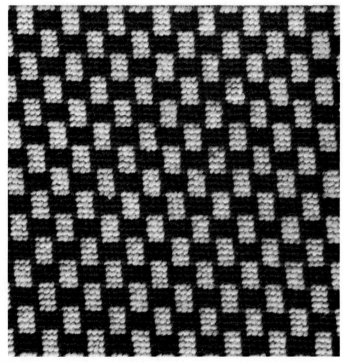

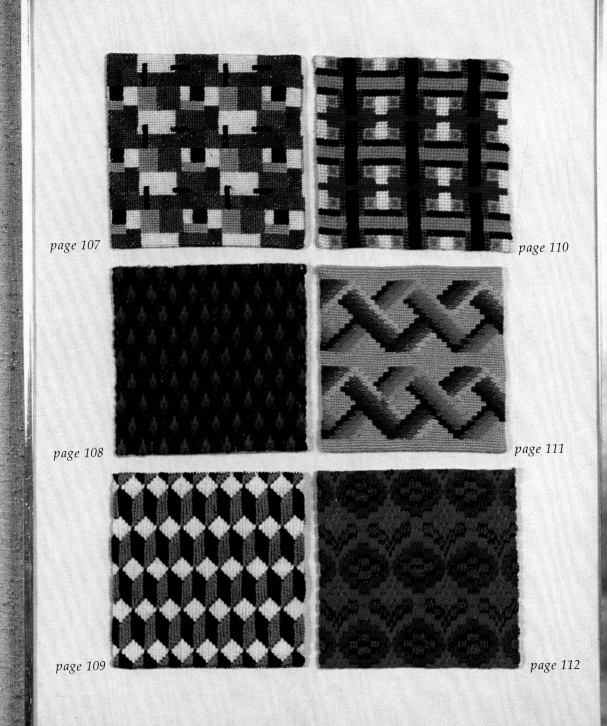

page 107

page 110

page 108

page 111

page 109

page 112

page 113

page 116

page 117

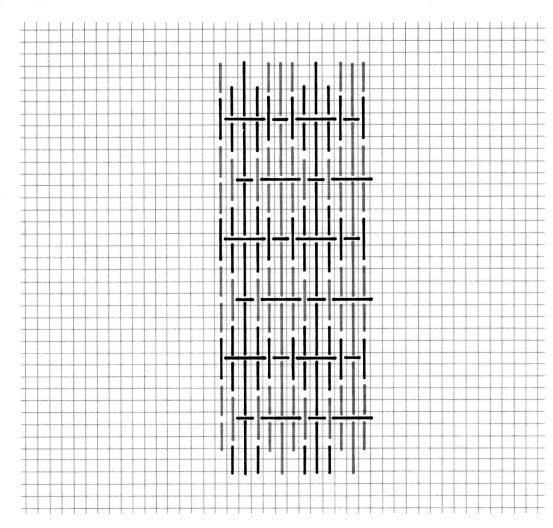

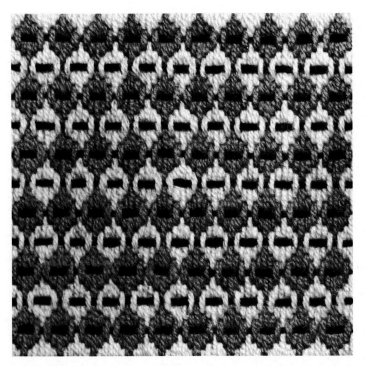

#10 Canvas
3-ply Persian-type Yarn
3 Colors

Work the horizontal rows
of diamond-like shapes,
one color at a time. Note
that the running stitch on
top of the work goes
under the outer stitches of
each diamond.

Color Illustration, page 115

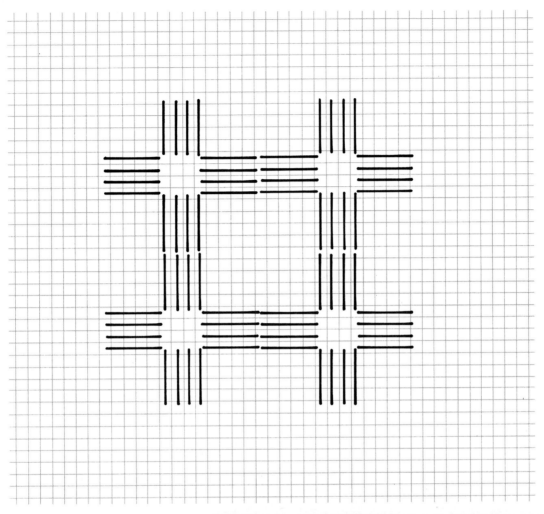

**#10 Canvas
3-ply Persian-type Yarn
4 Colors**

This pattern consists of straight stitches with a continental or basket-weave background. Work with 2 needles to establish one horizontal line of crosses. Then fill in the centers with French knots or cross-stitches. Finish the piece by working the background in the continental or basket-weave stitch.

Color Illustration, page 115

#12 Canvas
4-ply Tapestry Yarn
8 Colors

This pattern is done in
small straight stitches.
Work one diamond at a
time, connecting the
diamonds as you go
along. Then the cross
shapes will fall
automatically into place.

page 120

page 124

page 121

page 125

INTERMEDIATE

◢ = orange

• = green

#10 Canvas
3-ply Persian-type Yarn
2 Colors

Use the continental or
basket-weave stitch in
this grospoint pattern.
First establish the
complete framework in
one color. Then fill in the
second color.

Color Illustration, page 119

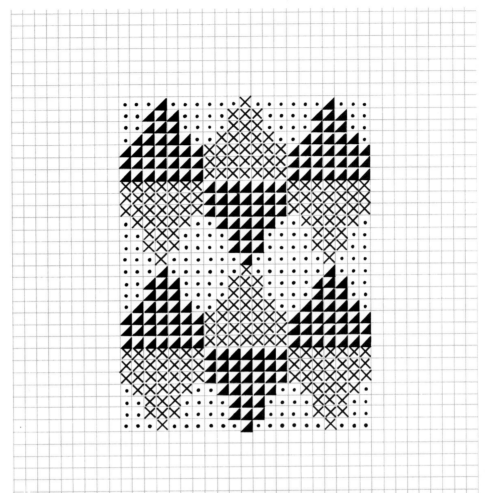

• = white
◢ = black
✕ = orange

**#5 Canvas
Quickpoint Yarn
3 Colors**

Try this easy one if
you've never done the
continental or basket-
weave stitch before.
First work the solid-color
diamond shapes across
the canvas. Then go back
with two needles and
work the triangles in the
two remaining colors.

Color Illustration, page 119

#10 Canvas
4-ply Tapestry Yarn
6 Colors

Look at this pattern as if
it were made up of
squares. Work each
complete square as a
unit, and the pattern
(including the center
flowers) will begin to fall
into place. At the center
of each flower place a
French knot in the
indicated color.

page 128

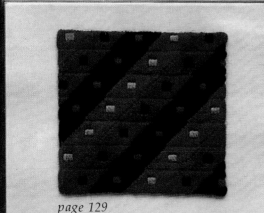
page 129

page 131

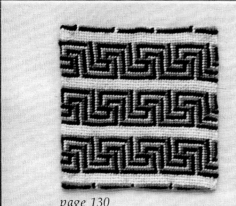
page 130

page 132

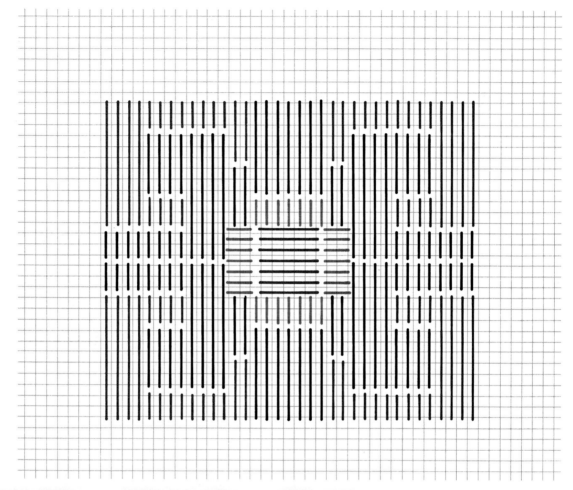

#12 Canvas
3-ply Persian-type Yarn
3 Colors

Another Indian-like
pattern, really very easy
to do if you count
carefully and concentrate.
Start with the center box.
To move to the next
repeat, work in a mirror
image.

Color Illustration, page 119

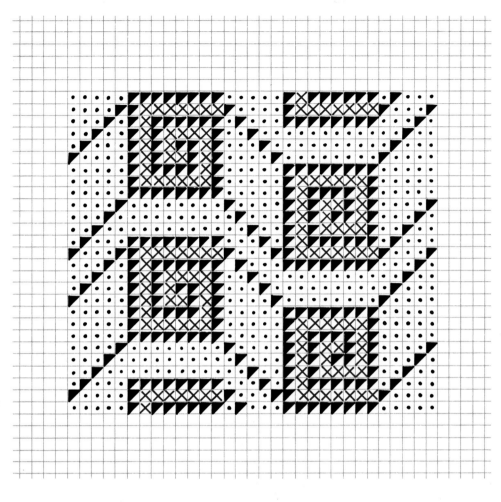

▲ = green
• = white
✕ = yellow

**#10 Canvas
4-ply Tapestry Yarn
3 Colors**

Done in the continental
or basket-weave stitch,
this is an unusual
grospoint design that is
easy but, like all such
patterns, requires careful
counting.

Color Illustration, page 119

page 133

page 136

page 134

page 137

page 135

page 138

page 139

page 140

page 141

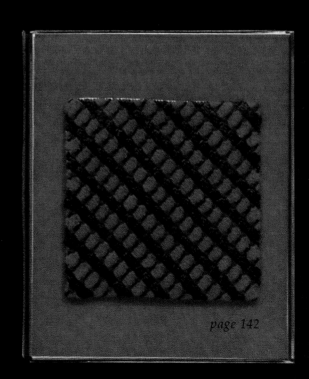

page 142

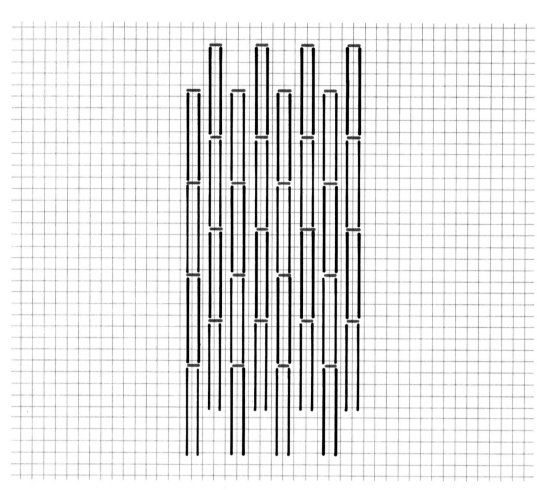

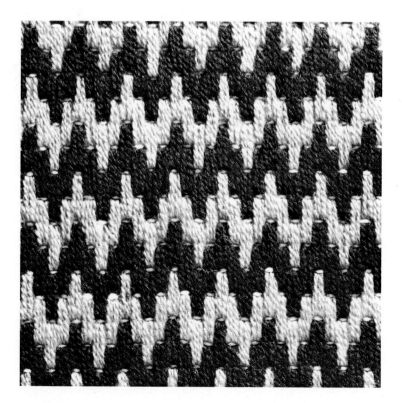

**#10 Canvas
3-ply Persian-type Yarn
3 Colors**

A very easy Bargello
pattern done in double
vertical stitches. Fill in
the horizontal running
stitch at the end.

Color Illustration, page 123

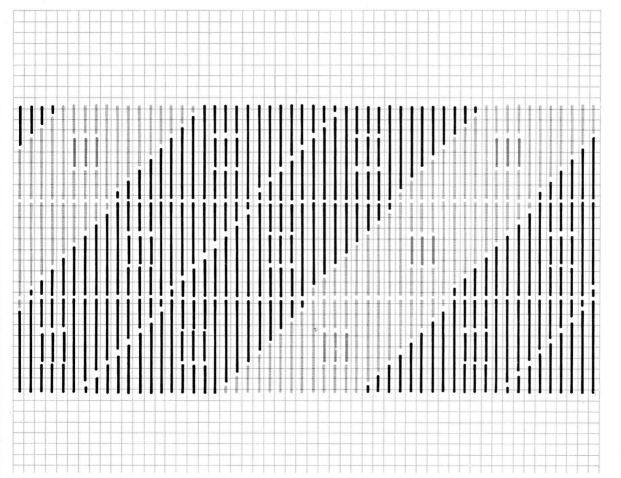

#12 Canvas
3-ply Persian-type Yarn
4 Colors

This is a very dramatic, optical pattern. Work on the diagonal, one shade at a time.

Color Illustration, page 123

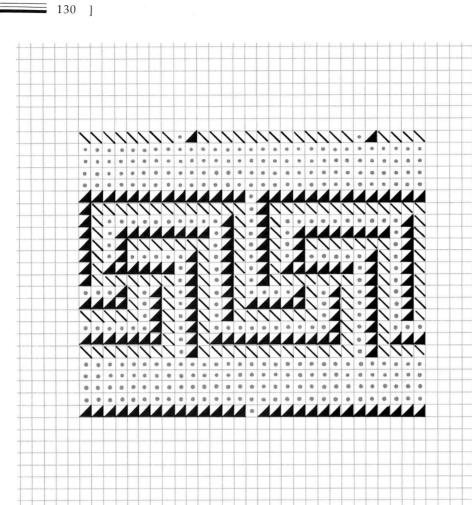

＼ = black
● = white
◢ = gray

#12 Canvas
4-ply Tapestry Yarn
3 Colors

A Greek-key grospoint pattern in the continental or basket-weave stitch. Work with three needles, establishing one key at a time all the way across the canvas. Then fill in the background.

Color Illustration, page 123

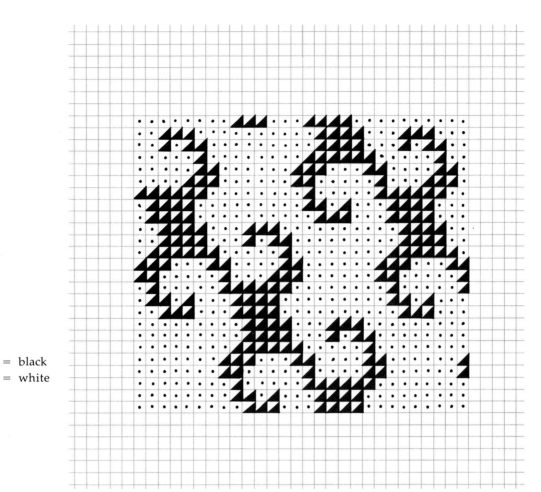

▲ = black
• = white

**#12 Canvas
4-ply Tapestry Yarn
2 Colors**

A traditional shape in grospoint that gives a contemporary-looking finished piece. First use the continental or basket-weave stitch to establish the connected "sea-horses" in diagonal rows in one color. Then fill in the background.

Color Illustration, page 123

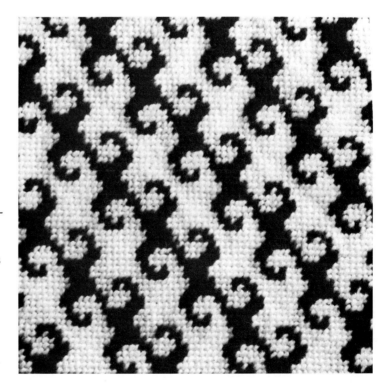

#10 Canvas
4-ply Tapestry Yarn
4 Colors

A very bold, geometric pattern. Work pattern diagonally, one shade at a time. This pattern has a tendency to pull out of shape. Allow extra canvas around the edge, as you may have to block more than once. Watch the right angles at the corners by counting carefully from the chart.

Color Illustration, page 123

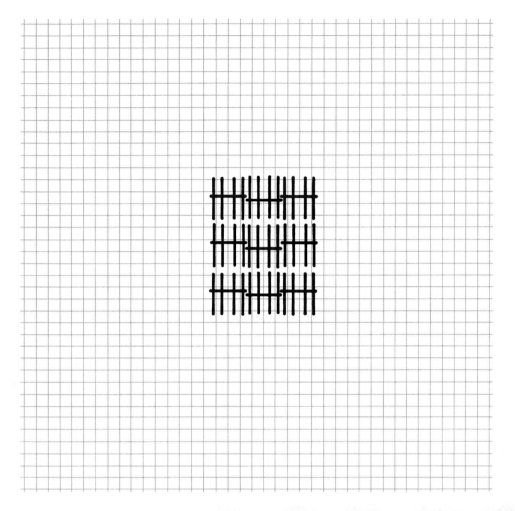

#5 Canvas
Quickpoint Yarn
2 Colors

A perfect pattern for
beginners. Work the
squares diagonally,
one color at a time,
completing each square
with a horizontal stitch
on top of the work.

Color Illustration, page 126

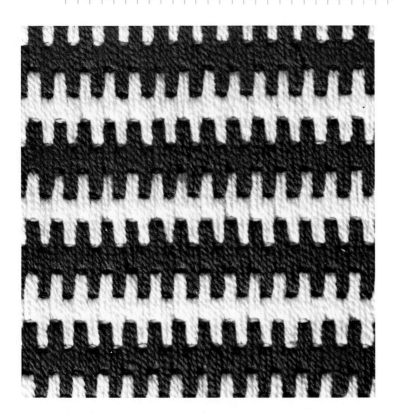

#10 Canvas
3-ply Persian-type Yarn
2 Colors

A very easy pattern,
perfect for beginners, or
for days when you'll be
talking a lot.

Color Illustration, page 126

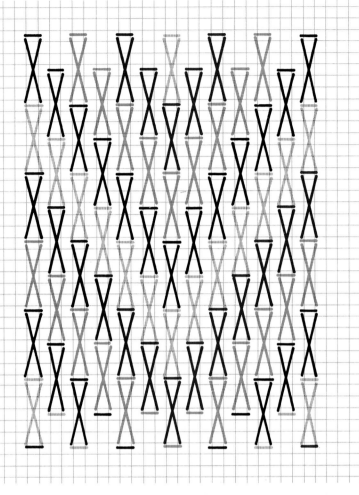

#10 Canvas
3-ply Persian-type Yarn
4 Colors

This pattern forms "V-shapes" with a long-legged cross-stitch. Work one complete cross-stitch at a time, making sure all the overlapping legs of the cross go in the same direction. Establish the "V-shapes" first. Fill in the short horizontal lines at the tops of the crosses when the rest of the work is finished.

Color Illustration, page 126

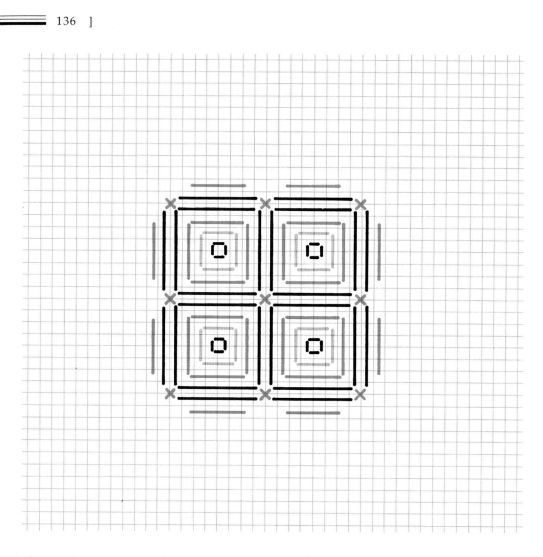

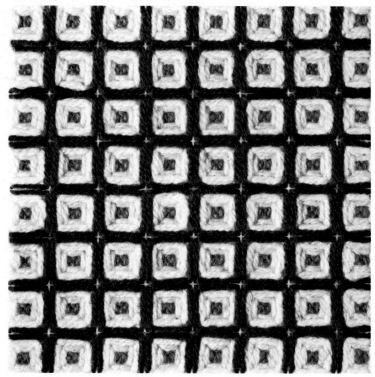

#10 Canvas
3-ply Persian-type Yarn
4 Colors

This is a pattern of
squares within squares
in 4 different sizes. First
do the largest squares
over the entire canvas.
Then do the next largest
squares, etc. Where the
corners meet, make a
small cross-stitch.

Color Illustration, page 126

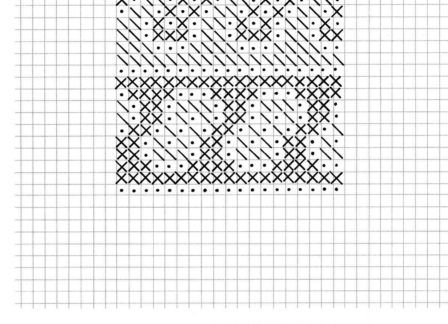

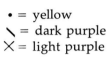

• = yellow
\ = dark purple
X = light purple

#10 Canvas
4-ply Tapestry Yarn
3 Colors

This pattern consists of horizontal rows in alternating background colors. Working with three needles in the continental or basket-weave stitch, complete one strip at a time, counting accurately.

Color Illustration, page 126.

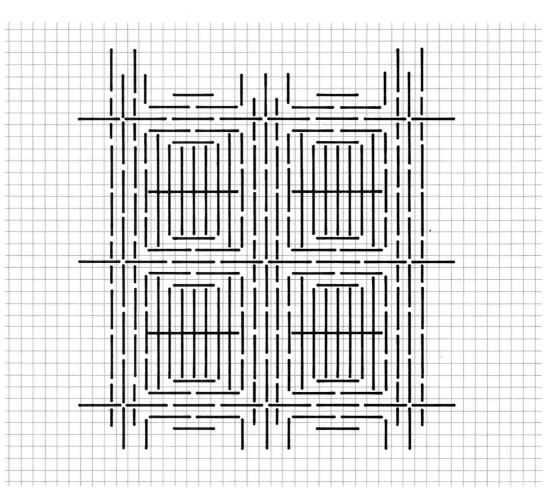

**#10 Canvas
3-ply Persian-type Yarn
2 Colors**

Work the vertical leaves
first. Then work the
horizontal leaves. By
this method, the flowers
will be formed and the
background will fall into
place. The horizontal
lines are laid on top of
the squares at the end.

Color Illustration, page 126

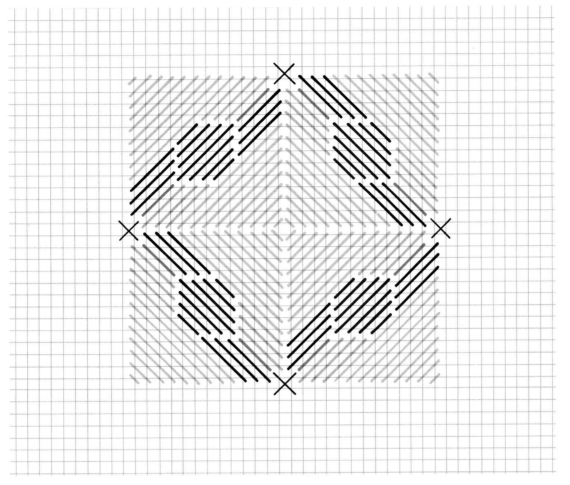

#10 Canvas
3-ply Persian-type Yarn
6 Colors

A very attractive pattern
that gives a quilted
effect. Look at the design
as if it were made up of
small squares with a
colored sash down their
middle. Work the squares
across the canvas in all
the colors they require.
Fill in the cross-stitches
at the end in another
color.

Color Illustration, page 127

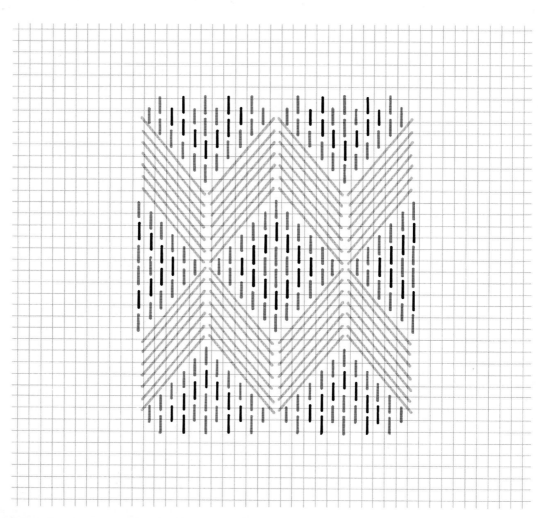

#5 Canvas
Quickpoint Yarn
3 Colors

A quickpoint pattern, combining Bargello and bold slanted stitches. First establish all the diamonds in horizontal rows. Then go back and fill in the slanted frame.

Color Illustration, page 127

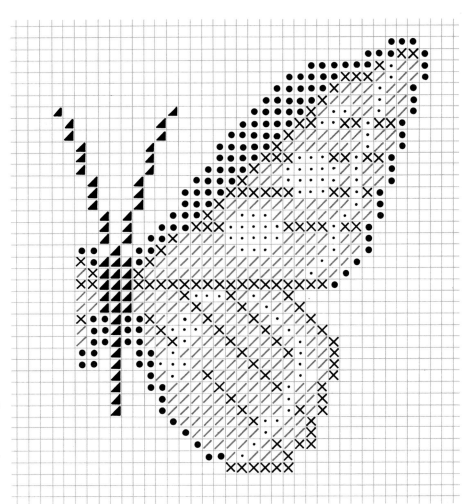

◢ = black
● = navy blue
✕ = medium blue
╱ = light blue
• = white
yellow background

#12 Canvas
4-ply Tapestry Yarn
5 Colors (plus background)

This butterfly is done in the continental stitch. It is easy if you are familiar with the stitch. However, it requires accurate counting from the chart, and you need to concentrate.

Color Illustration, page 127

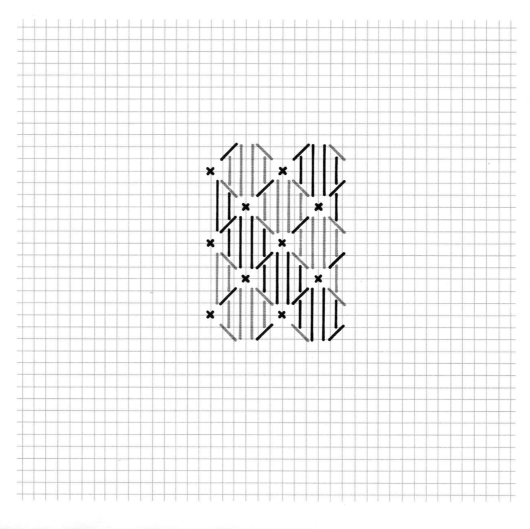

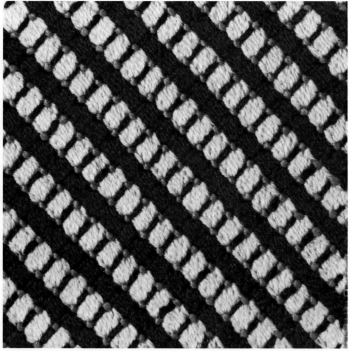

**#10 Canvas
3-ply Persian-type Yarn
3 Colors**

First work the diagonal
rows one color at a
time. Next outline each
box with straight
stitches. Finally, fill in
the cross-stitches at the
corners.

Color Illustration, page 127

ABOUT THE AUTHOR

LISBETH PERRONE is from an ancient and eminent Swedish family with a special interest in the arts. She spent her childhood surrounded by artists and craftsmen.

She studied in Paris and graduated with a degree in Decorative Arts from *Handabetets Vanner* in Stockholm, Sweden. She now lives in New York with her husband and son and teaches at the American Embroiderers' Guild, of which she is a Director.

Her work has appeared at the Smithsonian Institute in Washington, D.C. and in other museums. Articles about or by Lisbeth Perrone have been published in magazines in the United States and Europe.